How to Recognize Narcissism

Mila Gulliver

Contents

Chapter One

Introduction

Human psychology A difficult problem. Humans experience different traits that can be traced to their life experiences and genetic makeup. Every day a psychologist tries to understand the reasons why people do what they do. Many volumes have been published over the years showing the reasons for human actions. However, for many, personality remains a great mystery: narcissism. Narcissism is a personality trait that many have seen over the years. Although there are theories that attempt to explain why people exhibit narcissistic behavior, none of them solve the problem. To understand the problem of narcissistic abuse, we must first go back to the basics and understand narcissism. We need to better understand what narcissism is, what it does, and how it happens. Research shows how much misinformation exists about narcissism. The general concept of the subject is a core of incompatible and overly simplified concepts with a clear sense of "healthy" self-promotion, and it is not. Much of the negative rhetoric circulating online takes a black-and-white approach, as if narcissism is a pure and clear "label" rather than a collection of healthy and unhealthy reactions and behaviors shared by 98% of people (including you) who have. experienced It is very possible. This behavior occurs at different time periods with different intensities. Outcomes depend not only on basic, seemingly continuous mental processes, but also on what is currently (and recently) happening in life, which can exacerbate usually inactive self-esteem problems. Narcissism varies from low to high. Some narcissism is healthy, and some of our normal responses to threats to our ego allow us to protect our sense of identity without experiencing shame and failure. At the top of the scale is a personality disorder called narcissistic personality disorder (NPD), which is characterized by a sense of proud superiority, exaggerated gravity, and a deep sense of depth need for admiration

Chapter Two

What is narcissism?

The word Narcissism comes from the ancient Greek myth of Narcissus, a young man who was deceived by a demon and fell in love with his own reflection. He was so mad that he finally starved to death. Unfortunately, Nargis falls in love with Meditation and does not understand that he is not a real person. He died trying to achieve perfection. But the tragedy did not end there. The myth also includes a lesser-known character named Echo, a nymph with a unique curse: she can only repeat what others tell her.

He could not share his thoughts and feelings. One day he saw Nargis walking in the woods and his beauty immediately caught his attention. Although he tried to attract attention, his curse prevented him from communicating. Narges heard only the echo of her words. Echo's story also ends in disappointment. He finally died of a broken heart. Echo's story is familiar to anyone who has ever had a relationship with a narcissist. You try to express yourself, but your efforts fail. You rarely (if ever) feel seen or understood. Your point of view is ignored, your feelings are removed. As a weak echo, your efforts to communicate will fail. Sometimes you feel invisible, angry, depressed and humiliated. You get stuck in the struggle for recognition. When a narcissist looks lustfully in the mirror, one looks lustfully at the narcissist. But contrary to the simplicity of Greek myth, relationships with narcissists in the real world alternate with ups and downs. Unfortunately, when attachment alternates with periods of idealization and devaluation, you often experience joy and disappointment. What is narcissism? This word has a long and dark history. One hundred years ago, it was used to describe a kind of male sexual deviation. Since then, the term narcissism has been associated with many things, including developmental phase, way of relating to others, form of self-esteem regulation, trait or style, and personality disorder. Today, narcissism is a term often used in the context of narcissistic personality disorder (NPD). Personality disorders are characterized by persistent personality traits that cause problems in life and interpersonal relationships. In the case of NPD, these complex personality traits revolve around self-esteem issues. Unlike more focused diseases such as phobias or panic attacks, personality disorders usually affect several areas of life. Personality disorders can require long-term treatment and cause problems such as depression, anxiety, and drug abuse. Recent studies analyzing the results of a popular narcissism test, the Narcissistic Personality Survey (NBI), show that unhealthy narcissistic traits can be divided into three dimensions: chatter, selfishness, and pride. The book is organized using these three categories as a guide.What causes narcissism? Looking at the statistics, the figure of about one percent of the population with narcissistic personality disorder is incredibly high, perhaps embarrassing. At present, we have a broad and solid idea of who is generally interested in him. As we can see, narcissistic personality disorder is certainly not discriminatory, although certain criteria make a man more likely to develop the disorder, and it seems to be more common in men than women. Although we see people with narcissistic personality disorder or groups exhibiting most of their disorder, we have yet to discover a large number of underlying causes. The main purpose of this chapter is to analyze the various causes of narcissistic personality disorder and what can lead to the development of this terrible disorder. The exact causes of a narcissistic personality disorder are currently unknown. There are many indirect hypotheses about causal factors that lead to a common modern view of what causes the disease. The current agreement regarding the development of narcissistic personality disorder is that it is ultimately a combination of genetic, social, environmental, and biological factors. The exact role each plays in causing the disorder can vary from person to person, and the exact type of disorder caused will also vary. This means that there is no specific combination of factors that lead to the creation of a specific subgroup. "Why is this happening?" Dive into the big question. Also, let's take a look at each of them to get a more detailed understanding of the causes of narcissistic personality disorder. First, let's look at the genetic side: there is a lot of evidence that this disease can be inherited. Having a family member with the disorder increases their chances of developing the disorder. Repetitive studies have been sufficient to show that this disease has a hereditary origin. However, it is difficult to determine the extent to which a person grows up with a person with a disorder, for example, if their parent has a narcissistic personality disorder. This definitely results in the child absorbing this influence and being a bit annoying, and there are many environmental factors in addition to genetic factors. Here we will analyze the social and environmental catalysts for the development of a narcissistic personality disorder. Although environment and biology play an equal role, or even have a minor influence on biology, they are thought to play a more important role in the development of this disease than genetic or biological causes. One of the main catalysts for the development of a narcissistic personality disorder is when a child learns the manipulative behavior of his parents or friends. Manipulative parenting is widespread and, unfortunately, manipulative parenting styles have long gone unpunished. Developmental psychology and emotional abuse were widely discussed in the second half of the 20th century, and as a result, very unhealthy parenting practices still exist. Besides, it's not just parents. It depends on a person's general lifestyle. Unfortunately, because of the way manipulative behavior works, a manipulative person can surround themselves with people who can manipulate them and never have to change their behavior. That is why they can teach the child as a standard. As attitudes toward child development change dramatically in the 21st century, this topic is expected to become less and less of a problem as people discuss topics such as mental and emotional abuse and become more vocally acceptable topics. Until then it will be a very important catalyst. Another catalyst for narcissistic personality disorder is emotional abuse in childhood. Manipulative behavior and emotional abuse are not the same thing, but often go together. In the latter case, a narcissistic personality disorder can develop as a defense or defense mechanism. This can be one of the most difficult cases for psychological treatment because they deal with such deep trauma. This is comparable to trying to force people to justify their situation to others who have not experienced emotional abuse as children. However, this does not mean that narcissists have developed this as a defense or defense mechanism. In many people, this disorder is caused in other ways. For example, many people like to write that the child does not receive many compliments. However, as the child grows, many activities, if visible, are actively formed and permanently fixed in the brain. . , can cultivate a view of infallibility. Unfortunately, this often happens to single parents who do not want to lose the respect or admiration of their children, and we have seen many such cases. Similarly, if a child is criticized too often, they may develop narcissistic personality disorder as a defense mechanism. If people constantly tell someone that they are very handsome or talented without any basis in reality, or make severely realistic comments in response to compliments, they risk developing a narcissistic personality disorder. If people value them often or love them a lot, they are more likely to develop disorders. The mind prefers balance in interactions with others. Do your best to reach that balance and look for it. Believe it or not, not all minds are equally flexible and can easily tolerate certain stresses or excesses in life. In other words, many of the causes of narcissistic personality disorder can be traced to over-parenting. Someone who praises, criticizes, or overly manipulates a child risks you to develop a narcissistic personality disorder. Narcissistic parents often use their children as a means to determine their own fate and impose their narcissistic behavior on their children. This usually leads to reluctance or development of Stockholm syndrome. In the first case, people may stop communicating with their parents or even limit communication as much as possible. In the second case, they are often modeled after their parents. There is not much research on the biological factors associated with the development of this disease. As I said before, finding limited opportunities to study a narcissistic personality disorder can be difficult. However, studies show that the areas of the brain associated with empathy, emotion, and compassion tend not to be as large as in people without neurotics or psychosis. One of the questions many people reading this may ask is whether they can tell if their child is a narcissist or not. If you've already taken this book because you're worried that your child is suffering from this disorder, I have a pretty disappointing answer for you: your hypothesis is as good as mine. The fact is that although one of the factors associated with the development of narcissistic personality disorder is extreme sensitivity in childhood, it is one of the few symptoms that can be observed in the development of narcissistic personality disorder to adulthood. Many sensitive children do not suffer from this disease. That means we are a little lost on the specific answer. If you care that your child is a narcissist, check out his or her parenting style and learn about his or her family history. If others show signs of narcissistic personality disorder or praise your child too much without realistic suggestions or too much criticism, you may have a narcissist on your hands. However, many children and adolescents show signs of narcissism as a middle stage Eventually they give up. Their brains are developing and they have a lot to learn about the world. Depending on how young they are, just be reasonable about their age. If you are worried or your child has too many symptoms, it is a good idea to see a child psychiatrist for a professional evaluation. If you have been diagnosed with narcissism or a related mental disorder, your psychiatrist will work with you and your child to find a way forward.who is a narcissist A person with a narcissistic personality disorder is usually unhappy. These people are very gentle and can go wild if not taken care of. They want to get everything they deserve and try to get it by manipulation and force. Many people perceive narcissists as selfish and unloving. However, narcissism has deeper roots than selfishness. Narcissism is about taking what you think is yours, in any way possible. Narcissists do not pay much attention to the feelings and desires of others. Prioritize their needs and personalities. They get what they want, even if they step on someone. Although there are medical options for narcissism, the biggest challenge is patient acceptance. Narcissists do not think they are suffering from this disease. Even close people may not recognize a narcissistic person. A narcissistic person should seek help in cases where friends or family are aware of the symptoms of narcissism. Many of them consider themselves more and better than others. Narcissism is easily noticeable. Because this condition can harm more than the affected person, family and friends, everyone should be aware of its symptoms. Early detection of narcissistic behavior can help prevent harmful relationships or help the narcissist help.

The next We need to analyze some of the signs that the person you are with is a narcissist. Many narcissists work very well and hide well. Looking at them, it takes a little to get small things, and they may have a close relationship before finding narcissism, or before they understand anything. When you spend time studying the general definitions given by nurses or NPDs, it can be easily considered a narcissistic person who seems to be crucial or unpleasant or manipulated. We all talk about manipulation and perceive it as something negative, we all use manipulation in one way or another. So we have to spend some time analyzing what characterizes this person as a narcissist. According to the information contained in the diagnostic manual of the American Psychiatric Association, a person classified as a narcissist will have at least five traits, which we will discuss below. Narges exaggerates the importance. People who are narcissistic and NPD love others who think they are truly superior. While it's okay to want to get better while you're there, more often than not the narcissist doesn't have the results or skills to justify those feelings. They believe that their skills are better than theirs, so they try to minimize the skills and other contributions of others in any situation. You will often find that narcissists want to receive compliments from everyone they meet. And when they don't get such praise, the praise they somehow deserve can cause surprise and anger. Therefore, if Nargiz does not receive such recognition and success, it is time to blame others. This defect can be transmitted to the whole society, to another person or situation. Even if the narcissist thinks they are wonderful and unique, the responsibility is never on the narcissist. In the world we live in, there is nothing wrong with having a decent level of self-esteem and confidence in life. These may be the right things. But when we see a narcissist, they will probably take it to extremes. They often think that they are so unique and special that only other exceptional people can understand them. Therefore, narcissists want to surround themselves only with the best, and this can include the doctors they see and the friends they go with. For example, in the treatment of narcissism, it is shown how it should be understood only by an ideal person.They don't want to go to the first open therapist. They don't want to work with students and learners. Be assured that only the best can work with them. Narges always wants to praise him. Often, narcissists act with overconfidence and are very proud of the process. But even then their self-esteem is very low, which makes them delicate. Narcissists tend to care more about how others perceive them. Therefore, when they realize that those around them do not want to worship and admire, the narcissist is shocked and hurt and shows his disgust. This is very common in narcissistic people. Narcissus comes in and acts like he's newly in love with someone else he had a relationship with, but that only lasts until it's another compliment to Narcissus. Narcissists are sweet and can overwhelm the other person with emotion and attention (in a process known as bullying), but when the couple tries to protect themselves, everything goes away. We need to remember that narcissists admire others and expect them to be like them. So when others come back or have a different opinion, it can cause problems. In these situations, narcissists can become very angry, timid, and sometimes violent. Nargis is feeling better.When we look at a narcissist, we often see that he feels empowered to do things he is not allowed to do. These narcissists seem to be under the false belief that existing laws and regulations apply only to others and not to them. There are many ways a narcissist can present this, including disrespect to others, which should guarantee more respect. This can be seen when narcissists get angry and despise any authoritarian personality. You will also see a narcissist waiting for others to bend over and jump off the wheels. And when someone does all this, the narcissist will not appreciate any of their efforts. When we look into the mind of a narcissist, we see that it is quite reasonable for him to change his life around him and plan events etc around him. So if they pick him, no matter how hard they try, they won't show up. They think they can do it, everyone should accept it and not be nervous or bothered at all. A narcissist struggles with any form of empathy for others. Often the narcissist is known for not being able to understand or comprehend the pain, struggle, or emotions of others. There are times when this person seems right Fair and intelligent. But they say something incredibly insensitive about why it hurts others and makes them do it. Narges is very jealous. Many narcissists like to compare themselves and their lives with others. Often they choose not neighbors or friends, but successful and famous people. This can be even worse for narcissists because it increases their jealousy. If they succeed in life, they happily believe that others will envy or envy them as well. A narcissist is often proud and arrogant. When they were sweet and delicious, you can easily choose the best wine from the list and have to be wrong for the server? This is a sign that we must be careful about the wrong story, and it can be a sign that one is some other symptoms we are talking about. Narges is like that and even manages to pull him out of the restaurant. They act like arrogant, wise and innocent people, while everyone else is ignorant and erroneous. If you start noticing these traits in the person you spend time with, that person is most likely a narcissist. Narcissus devotes time to successful fantasies and finds the right combination. A narcissist often spends a lot of time thinking about how to gain the respect, success and favor of others. There are three things about influencers that make them happier. It plays an important role in many areas of your life, including how you choose the person with whom you sometimes want to be romantically involved. Some research has been done on this topic and it helps to see how narcissists tend to emphasize things like physical attractiveness and status more than any other traits or personalities. The narcissist does not care about these later aspects. This is because the narcissist believes that when their partner feels good, they can boost their self-esteem and help Sherbet feel better. Narcissists often benefit from others. If you combine the lack of empathy and the law of narcissism, you will see that they can easily take advantage of those around them without making them feel bad. And they will do so with anyone, at any time, as long as they give the narcissist an advantage along the way. Because narcissists believe they have the right to get what they want and act the way they want, they use what they want, without caring or understanding how others feel. This is one of the reasons why it can be difficult to work with someone who is a narcissist or NDP. If you work with a narcissistic boss, he will try to help you with that and will often recognize, compensate or respect your work without guilt, even outside narcissists can take advantage of you in the workplace. There is often a strange friendship or relationship where one person is not afraid to get angry or try to do what they want. It's like that friend who's always too busy to spend time with you until you find something you like. You know they've always messed up, but they come back and try to use you. There are many aspects to consider when looking at someone who might be a narcissist. A person who exhibits one or both of these traits is sometimes not so important. But when a person exhibits these traits regularly and exhibits five or more of them, we can be sure that the person is a narcissist. What is the advantage of this? . Support your partner. Types of daffodils and how to recognize themNarcissism manifests itself in different ways, so there are different types of narcissism. You can classify narcissists according to how they behave in relationships or according to traits they often exhibit. In this section, we will look at the top five types of narcissism. If you spend a lot of time with a narcissist, you may exhibit personality traits that fall into several of the types we will discuss in this section, but if you want to understand what a specific type the narcissist is, no matter what you are. , always accept its most defining features. dominant Here are the five main types of narcissists you will encounter sometime in your life :

Junkie

When a narcissus Human abuse is not always the fault of the victim. Because everyone can be deceived and become an emotional victim. Basically, every person is sensitive and vulnerable to all kinds of toxins. It is important to know the traits that narcissists seek to protect themselves and avoid. This is when a potential victim reaches a point where they realize they are being exploited or attacked. It is known that their quality is best when they can be used positively. For an evil narcissist, their personality will rule, but unfortunately they use it against someone else. mentally ill, Mently ill, mensmalsanaSadistic type. This type of narcissist is often confused with psychopaths and people with other antisocial personality disorders. They do not regret and are not interested in moral or immoral behavior. His self-esteem is proud and expensive. They want to make fun of others. Mostly these are thugs in prisons or drug rehabilitation facilities. They are known for humiliating others for unconventional sexual reasons.exhibitorThey are less sensitive, but safer. They consider themselves superior and always take revenge or anger against people who disrespect them or dare to make negative comments. This group does not feel ashamed and has high self-esteem. They come from the benefits they received when their parents felt better than when they were children. Unlike sensitive narcissists, they simply act as expected from childhood. They don't care how others feel about them and can quickly leave a conversation if they don't get the praise or respect they deserve. If they are in a relationship, they don't care about their partner's feelings, and if they don't get recognition, they can quickly leave the relationship. They will obviously have a lot of relationships and are not proud of how people see them or how great they are.

They can be very dominant and very aggressive when analyzing problems. annoyingThese narcissists operate on the assumption that the other is constructed by breaking or removing them. The purpose of intimidation is to assert superiority, and this kind of narcissist is ruthless in how he does it. We are not talking about school stalker: the narcissistic stalker is more complex (his methods may resemble those of school stalker). This kind of narcissist treats others with contempt, makes them feel like failures, and allows them to feel successful. Someone watching you every step of the way will throw cold water on all your efforts to improve. Your criticisms are never constructive: they are meant to make fun of you and tell you that it cannot be improved or appreciated. If this type of narcissist wants something from you, they don't want it. He hears it; Sounds like what you need. witchThey are narcissists who tend to manipulate people for their own benefit. Unlike other narcissists, they actually feel good about you, but that feeling doesn't last long: it ends when they succeed. Subconsciously, they start to express admiration to you, but it's always what they think they want to hear, and they give them the same compliment so they can use you. When seducers get what they want from you, they reveal their true colors and pull the rug under their feet. Such a man can still give compliments, but when he fulfills his request, they begin to repay him. If you're dating someone who flatters you all the time, try to see if they do the same with others. If the service is only directed at you, it is because they indicate manipulation.

Chapter Three

Effects of narcissistic bullying

Emotional Manipulation is one of the signs of narcissistic abuse. Narcissists use language to blame their partner or someone else for challenging their feelings or reality, making them feel that you are to blame, not the narcissist. In a sense, narcissistic bullying is a way of controlling thoughts through language to induce guilt, regret, paranoia, doubt, and other mental / emotional states. Abuse is a form of psychological and emotional manipulation in which the victim of abuse questions their desires, opinions, personal autonomy, etc., in order to achieve the narcissist's priorities and goals. How to Survive Being a Victim of Narcissistic Bullying: You Can Challenge Your Mental Health. You may find that you don't trust the people who support you in life, like family and friends. The narcissist is the only person who cares about you and loves you, and you can be sure that others have abandoned you. Feeling worthless refuses to accept any hard work because you know your narcissistic partner is just despising you. He doubts whether he will be able to make the right decisions or think clearly and effectively. Complete disconnection of personal desires and needs. Whatever you want, do everything you can to get the support of your narcissistic partner by controlling your thoughts and beliefs about yourself. Obsessing over every failure or mistake you think you have made will help you get better on a regular basis. He denies

Nargis and apologizes for his behavior. Be better than your narcissistic partner who has mentally "trained" you to do this. Obsessive thoughts about how to please them. These situations do not always occur and are signs of mental and emotional manipulation by the narcissist. Even before you realize that you are being bullied and emotionally manipulated, it manifests itself that way and is very subtle and can happen for a long time. Let's create an example of what that looks like in everyday life. A victim of narcissistic abuse may feel uncomfortable, insecure, emotionally upset, and disconnected from their true feelings during their first therapy sessions. He is here today because his partner has shown him that if he wants to be in society, he has a problem and needs help. He can excite his failures and failures and talk about his shortcomings and the need to improve his problems and failures his partner told him. This may happen that he does not meet his partner's needs correctly and does not meet his expectations, that is, he is not enough for him and is very concerned about children, excludes him or no sexual act. The victim constantly wants to understand why she can't satisfy her partner and tells him that she doesn't understand why he still doesn't meet her expectations. He doesn't even know he's feeding it and creates a reality in which he has to doubt himself in order to survive. You can ask him why he is unhappy or solid. At that moment, he tells him that he was unhappy, uncertain and ridiculed and ridiculed him. During the medical session, the victim can start expressing the ideas of hatred, condemnation and image, as well as the image of his worthless man, who is not a good companion and how to entertain him. These include defensive statements that acquit the partner of guilt, another symbol of the narcissist's power and control. Reports may include some of the following:We come together a lot and I really enjoy it and we laugh a little. I just a few little things. No major problems I know it's my fault and I'm the only one who needs to change. Can you help me become a better partner? Please help me understand how I can continue to bother you. I can't lose it, I have to figure out how to fix it. I know it's my fault, so where do I start loving me? Do you think there is hope for improvement? Such repeated statements or cycles and mindsets are just the tip of the iceberg about how psychological and emotional abuse manifests. It's a long and difficult road of constant manipulation and emotional abuse that deceives your mind into believing that you have an individual personality disorder. Here are a few more examples of how this narcissistic tactic manifests itself in victim abuse: The word "failure" is often used to describe their inability to support their partner. (e.g. I can't love him more or feel safer). You can't "learn" to fix it or improve it without your partner being hurt or hurt. And he can't do anything that can cause problems, for example, calling him to shout at him, questioning him, punishing him. He is confused as to how he can be so agitated or "crushed" over "little things". If you resist your partner's demands or set boundaries, this is called "madness" and you may need professional help or medication. He can blame himself for causing problems in his relationship and wants to know what he can do to stop it. The victim believes what the narcissist said: that if something is wrong in their relationship, it is their fault and needs to be fixed and improved. Emotional violence is the way Narges keeps his partner in the soul, which allows you to continue, as it does in life, and how they are in a long -term relationship with a partner. It is not always aggressive, threatening or attacking, but a delicate and strategic purpose of believing that the victim is not bold and cannot do much work to keep him in poor conditions and in extreme mood, mood and mood. Like, some symptoms of mood were expressed as after -traumatic stress or disorder. Some, but not all, of these symptoms can trigger thoughts and memories that appear out of nowhere. Emotional and physical reminders of traumatic or traumatic moments. Awakening experiences in your mind or night dreams. Negative, sad and negative thoughts about yourself or the world. Strange or strange that the concentration of insomnia, insomnia, or excessive awareness of the feeling separated from others in your life, this method usually results with a storm that allows you to talk about a wonderful love for your partner's bombardment and speed, even eyes that loves his companion, even eyes who love their partner. And at the beginning of a journey, the signs of nature did not show his care. There is an important reason for this: Narcissus does not want you to know that he will treat you later, and often he doesn't even know it. She has not yet reached the point in the relationship where she no longer satisfies the needs of the goddesses of love and narcissism, so at first there are no visible signs that emotional abuse is hiding around the corner. It may take weeks, months, or even a year to realize that you haven’t aged or who you were when you first fell in love with them. Your friends may notice that you have changed and act as if you are not the same, and then you can tell them what your narcissistic partner would believe you: "We surprise each other because we fight so hard." "We're good." and we will come later. We're so in love that I can't see my life without him. " He wants everything in a certain way. Who can blame him? When you go into the hiding place of emotional abuse, your apologies pile up and you end up believing everything your partner tells you and doing everything you can to convince those around you that you are happy and ready to cooperate. Make your life happy. Narcissists repeatedly show you how to think, feel, and act around them, and you come to understand that everything they say or think about you must be true. It's like hating each other and doubting the process. This is how emotional abuse works. Unexpectedly posted in comments or sarcastic remarks. While your partner is reassured to be better, he looks awkward in public and in front of others. It replaces any inner confidence and knowledge and turns one's self-confidence into doubt and an inability to reflect on one's lives and circumstances. Narcissists have power over you and can rule you Mind, will and personal beliefs about themselves and the world through emotional tactics. Here are other examples of their narcissism: to prevent oral abuse and delays of toxic punishment (creating unnecessary emotions or emotions to another person) (refusing to talk directly to you to create attack It is very difficult. A narcissistic aggressor has a lot of experience in manipulating situations, events and facts according to his needs and can put you in the place of violence with both bombs and sweet wars or arguments to convince the victim after the aggressive act. It is not illegal. They can use tactics to convince you that you are abusing it. The following symptoms are some of the most common side effects of emotional abuse. For this to happen, your partner does not have to be a narcissist. However, the psychological manipulation tactics used by the narcissist often accompany these symptoms. Go survive To dissociate means to separate or separate something. In situations of emotional abuse, you may need to completely isolate yourself from the environment. This type of attachment can affect your personality and sense of self, your perception of reality, your memory and awareness. It's a way to sleep from the trauma of being bullied. Feeling uneasy about maintaining the status quo can include repeated reckless actions, addictions, and a natural obsession with things or events. That way you can escape from the reality of life. That way your mind can block anything that is emotionally harmful or painful so that you don't have to deal with all the facts and truths about the realities of your relationship. Isolation is a common factor in violent situations. How many people find out who they are and what they want long enough to preserve that reality in a particular society that allows them to exist or live in the current reality. Stroll on eggshells In a traumatic situation, whether traumatic or not, the goal is to avoid re-experiencing or reproducing one of those traumas. Narcissistic bullying, although subtle and hard to detect, is harmful. When you are afraid to touch the bees or lift the sleep of a bear, you can walk in eggs. This means that you are very careful about everything you can tell you to avoid all your actions, anger or approaches and unpleasant behavior. In general, walking is not a solution to an egg because you can find a way to find a disability or misunderstanding of their behavior. Walk in an egg -nests is associated with your relationship and measures outside this forum, and you will have problems with the valuation of the outside world, because you are always careless and careless without anyone or anyone.Ignore the body, the victim's significant feelings and needs by the perpetrator. Whatever you meet your needs, you may notice that your relationship or influence of narcissism, make sure your partner is happy and can be a complete task. When you are deeply involved, you become a guard please make your partner happy and sacrifice your full time and energy to meet all your needs. It can get worse over time and lead to minor problems such as emotional distress, pain or physical symptoms, and neglect of basic health needs. A narcissist will never be happy no matter how his needs are met, so he tragically loses himself when he gives himself over to everything. Health and mental health problems. Maintaining the last critical point, your engagement can eventually lead to more serious problems. Lack of self -improvement to make another person happy can lead to deep pain, which begins to express both physically, mentally, and both! When you are not in the right balance with you, your physical health may worsen and you can often get sick or cause chronic problems that are not away from your doctor. This can be a This is a good sign that your physical illness is usually related to mental illness. Psychiatric problems often appear in situations of abuse and can include depression, insomnia, anxiety, paranoia, obsessive-compulsive disorder, mental and emotional exhaustion, and more. Because you've never had these problems before, you may be wondering where these problems come from. Of course, the last person to accuse him was his attacker. This is where cycles and patterns of bullying get stuck over and over again. You need to honestly ask yourself why you have health and mental health problems. Narcissistic abuse is probably the cause. The general distrust associated with flaming is a common tactic of narcissistic abusers. Gasification is a psychological manipulation aimed at questioning a person's mental health. Tried so often, he finds it hard to trust anyone, especially his accuser. As you slowly and gradually “learn” to question your own sanity or sanity, it will be difficult for you to trust the other person and their claims. He may even lose the ability to believe in himself and believe that his thoughts and experiences must be wrong or wrong. There are thoughts or motivations to harm oneself, and the pain of abuse, whether it occurs or not, can cause an endless cycle of depression, anxiety, and despair. These situations eventually become unbearable and there is no hope of getting rid of the pain or the current situation. Her attacker may have used cunning and submissive means to convince her that she was vulnerable and unsavable if she tried. This kind of thinking creates a need to escape, manipulates emotions into self-harm or self-harm, and can even lead to suicidal thoughts. Isolation Sometimes a narcissistic partner creates an environment where they are both isolated and in their own tiny world, so they cannot be bothered or questioned. In some other cases, the victim of abuse usually isolates themselves due to shame or feelings of isolation. With no way to escape or explain the status of the forum, it is easier to fall apart than to seek help and find a solution. Withdrawal from others seems like the safest choice, especially after the perpetrator has convinced you that you are mentally ill and should not trust your instincts. Do what you love, without fear of failure. Narcissists are often jealous of others, including their partners or victims of abuse. Maybe something unusual will happen in your life to feel the punishment of your attacker. A narcissistic abuser psychologically forces his partner or victim to look at his success negatively and see it as a problem rather than something to be proud of. This can lead to depression, anxiety, low self-esteem, self-doubt and many other symptoms. It's almost impossible to thrive and do what you love in an environment of bullying. Protect your abuser and enlighten yourself when these patterns are fixed and if you are in a "comfortable" relationship between the abuser and the victim, you will be forced to rationalize your relationship, minimize the problems and deny Concern about their relationship for any reason. . It is usually said that everything you did to provoke your partner was your fault and you should know. It is easy for abusers to demand moments of magic and reconciliation so that they do not lose love. This maneuver perpetuates the attack cycle and provides a narcissistic advantage. All of these situations can fall on the attractive spectrum depending on the relationship.

Not all narcissistic stories involve such extreme or intense psychological and emotional abuse. If you've read this chapter and feel that your partner is hurting you, it's time to start identifying things you can change or seek help. You cannot change the actions and behavior of a narcissist, so you must be prepared to be in such a toxic situation..

An A strong traumatic bond is created between the criminal and the victim. This is because the criminal thus "prepares" the victim, and the victim chooses survival tactics. In a violent relationship, the victim shares responsibility for the abuse. Are you blaming yourself for relationship dramas? Is your partner responsible for your problems or actions? What should I do now? If you're in a relationship that's good, don't be afraid. No matter how lonely you feel, you are not alone. Many who find out what is happening or what has happened are being persecuted. Asking for help begins with identifying problems. The first step is to become aware of your situation and the reality in which you have been and validate your feelings and experiences. Your abuser may be trying to manipulate your thoughts and ideas or scare you, but if you want to get out of the cycles and patterns of bullying and heal the wounds they have caused, you still need to identify the problem. If you're not ready to confront your partner about what you think is happening in your relationship, start writing it down. Take a notebook or journal with you and write down any events or experiences. Compare this information with some of the signs and symptoms of narcissistic bullying that you read in this book. If you can, find a therapist or clinical social worker you trust and share your truth with them. Tell some family members what's going on in your relationship. Talk to friends and loved ones who don't have the experience and can give their perspective. In your experience journal, you can begin to work on your feelings and discover patterns and cycles of abuse created by your partner. You can also try other treatments, especially if you are experiencing physical or emotional symptoms. Leaving this type of relationship can be very difficult, especially if the relationship is harmful. Although there are cycles of abuse, there are many reasons why people do not want to leave their partners. However, the important part of everything, and the reason to read this book, whether you are a victim of narcissistic abuse or in a relationship with a narcissist, is to learn how to heal and live a healthy and prosperous life. You can also have kids to think about, and you want the best for their happiness and health. In the next section, you will find more information about the effects of narcissistic parents on children. You may also be the son of a narcissist, so there may be other types of narcissists this season Information.Chapter 4. The cycle of fraudIdealizationIdealization occurs when the narcissist or abuser puts you on a pedestal. He says how wonderful you are, how he can't live without you and how important you are to him. This level usually includes a lot of gifts for you and relates to the emotional level. You feel loved, valued, desired and you live with that feeling. This is the stage you can't wait for. It also links you to four other steps, even fewer. It means a whirlwind of romance, charm, love, admiration and praise. This situation is often accompanied by promises about the future, such as marriage, buying a house or children. The claims presented here are intended to attract your desires and make you want to continue the relationship. At this stage, you should feel desired and emotionally dependent. Think about the wedding: This is the stage of the wedding. Only then does it seem that everything is seen and experienced in a new light. If you've been through this cycle before, the idealization stage can be daunting because you know what to expect. While you want to feel loved by them, you also risk hurting your partner. You know that the slightest offense and trying to avoid it leads to humiliation. Do your best to be kind and thank your partner.For example, imagine Anna and Eric's wedding. Eric is a narcissist. At that point, Eric sings Anna's praises. Knowing her phone is broken, he calls her, gives her jewelry and buys a new phone. He is attentive, gentle and seems the perfect companion. Anna is surprised at this stage of the relationship, falls in love and hopes this time will be different. She does her best to be a good wife and make sure her clothes are ready. He makes sure the dinner is ready and is intimate with her. He knows that her personality can sometimes explode, so she tries to avoid teasing him or doing anything that might upset him. Love and romance fade with time. Although they can still communicate regularly, and this is mostly positive, the constant flow of love will begin to fade and ensure a healthy relationship. Anna was not worried, for she had seen the outflow and flow of salt during the mating. devalueIn the devaluation stage, the abuse begins to creep back into the relationship. Come back as if nothing has changed. When your partner yells at you for small mistakes that don't matter in the big picture, you can start with verbal abuse — even buying the wrong oil that costs an extra $ 0.39 is likely to bother your partner. Your partner may accuse you of intentionally holding the ball. He accuses you of wanting to fight. So you can see the gas light aimed at convincing him that he is wrong about his understanding of events. If cheating is a problem in your relationship, he may cheat on you again or fight for a bet or drink more than you bargained for. At this point, your partner wants you to stay calm as the tension grows. Silence means accepting the narcissist and cooperating with him if necessary. He wants to teach you to endure resentment and keep calm. I mean you have narcissism. At this point, you can either escalate your actions by calling the narcissist about any abuse you are doing, or you can remain silent. No option is ideal, but at the end of the day you need to keep your limits. At this point, you can defend yourself and if you feel disrespected, you are allowed to leave temporarily or permanently. As for Anna and Eric, Anna could see that Eric's clothes smelled of perfume again and she physically wanted him less. When he says he wants to spend time with her, he constantly accuses her of being sticky or destitute and starts calling him when he cheats on her. Even if he has done nothing wrong, he finds a way to blame her for his bad character. Maybe he left the stove too high or forgot to wash the shirt he wears every Friday. Whatever you choose, you will have plenty to choose from. WasteThen comes the stage of rejection. This usually happens if you refuse to confess to the abuse. If you criticize the narcissist for their behavior, demand respect, or believe that you will not be deceived, they are likely to be offended. Remember, the worst thing a narcissist can imagine is to completely reject, ignore, and reject you, so that's exactly what he's going to do to you. He decides to get rid of you, hoping to teach you a lesson, and he thinks you will do the same. The condition of the injuries often needs to be treated or left alone. He may break up with you or refuse to acknowledge your existence. He believes he does not tolerate bullying, You respected him, and even if his mockery hurt you, they were expected to keep boundaries. After all, you are not cheated or called names in a relationship. You have the right to protect your boundaries and stop using narcissists. At this point, Anna is able to tell Eric that she knows about the adventure that awaits her. You can see him checking the news on his phone, or catch a glimpse of the other girl's hair in his clothes while washing, and the lipstick stains on the neck of that shirt he insists on looking great over the weekend. not to be After taking the keys, coat and phone, Eric responds by pointing to the clue and calls her, saying he disagrees with the treatment and betrayal. He reads the messages as he writes to him, judging by the tiny "read" news below everyone, but doesn't respond. It's peaceful. Hours become days, and he refuses to communicate with his wife. At that point, he begins to worry, but does not acknowledge his presence. She knows he works every day, but every time he connects to his office line, he disconnects from her. This situation makes Annan feel weak and unimportant. He tries to say it doesn't matter if he doesn't like it, he throws it away like garbage. Either way, the rejection phase ends, and depending on what you do, the relationship revolves around destruction or desire. If Anna does not continue her protest, the link will be empty. If he continues to label his behavior, he will most likely act destructively. destroyIf the period of denial ends in a confrontation or if you continue to engage in narcissistic behavior, the next stage is extinction. Then everything explodes. The narcissist explodes and the violence continues to escalate. It can be physical or sexual, or it can include threats. In any case, this condition forces you to give in emotionally and physically. By choosing regular patterns of use, narcissists intensify their behavior and do not stop. He will do whatever it takes to hurt you because he wants to make you suffer the pain you apparently caused him. He is deeply hurt and wants to hurt you as much as he does, even if he sees himself as a victim because of his distorted perception of reality. This is reason enough to justify his actions. During this abuse, you can physically isolate him by locking him somewhere or removing his keys, phone, money or anything else you can contact. This situation is about a narcissist who insists on controlling her. He thinks of his partner and blames him. This situation is the worst in terms of the damage done in the cycle of abuse. This can be explosive, dangerous and can lead to someone's death if allowed to continue or if the narcissist chooses not to stop. This is a very important part of the relationship, especially if the narcissist is usually physically violent. Not everyone does, but those who do are very dangerous during this period. To help, he wants to make sure you're stuck and make you wonder what happened and why it's your fault. After a long stint with his partner, Eric is able to return home with Anna. He came to show that he could come and go as he pleased, and Anna said anything. When he tells her she will end the relationship if he doesn't deal with it, she physically attacks him and challenges him and his actions. It moves him in a way he has never done before. Although it does not destroy anything or cause constant damage, it does leave marks on it. He tries to make a phone call and decides to take it and crush it, he owns it and does whatever he wants. After a long sentence, he took the key and left her alone in the room, leaving a brief explanation of what had provoked him. dust collectorThe state of desire takes its name from emptiness and relates to the fact that the narcissist is trying to attract it. He will know that he has seriously messed up the relationship, especially if he sees that you are not trying to keep in touch, and he will try to do so instead. At this stage, he will decide to plead guilty. He blames you or other external reasons. He may claim that he is ill, stressed or under the influence of drugs and alcohol, and therefore believes that he is not at fault. At this point, it's a sacrifice and nothing else matters. He can say that he is very sorry and promises to do better. He's probably crying and saying you're the best he's ever had and he can't believe he messed it up. The important thing to remember is that you don't want to say anything about it This is. He says he will do everything he can to keep it and bring it back. He does not regret what he has done and wants to make sure he is ready for a relationship with her. Maybe you don't want to deal with a divorce case, or you want to avoid moving or losing children, but for whatever reason, you want to take it seriously. At this stage, there may be signs of forgiveness: a chic gift, a heartfelt letter (but not because the narcissist doesn't like it), an apology, and doing something for yourself that you wouldn't normally do. He wants you to think that he is doing everything to agree to continue the relationship. Eric arrives and apologizes to Anna, who gives him a new one after he destroys the old one in a rage.You can see that this time he has taken a high-end model and, if he wants, offers a takeaway dinner at his favorite restaurant. At this point, she is ready to do what she wants and test the waters to make sure she wants to stay. If he says he is leaving, he will not defend himself now, but he can cry and apologize. He promises to go to therapy, recover, and end his relationship with another woman. Of course it's a lie, but we can expect him to say enough for Anna to believe. After a while, assuming he goes to therapy and the relationship ends, he may decide to try again. He says he's going to go the next time his relationship works, and he agrees that's just fair. After achieving the desires, the relationship returns to the stage of idealization. You've heard time and time again that everything is in order and everything will work out in your relationship, but you never suspected that your partner could do what he did. You're worried that you might hit again, and even though you're enjoying the moment, you can't relax. At this stage, the narcissist behaves normally for at least some time and does what he promises. He will not deceive you, hurt you, shout at you or do anything he promises.

However, it never lasted. As before, you end up doing something or blaming something, and in response to the threat, the relationship returns to devaluation. Cycles can last for weeks, months or even years, or happen almost every day. Finally, there are no clear guidelines on how far a person can go in a cycle of bullying. However, it is clear that violence always returns and is almost always worse than before. At the end of the day, whether you choose to stay in or out of the cycle of abuse is your choice. Remember that there are resources available to help people who live in fear of violence or serious violence. If you want, you can enter such a relationship, and you can find support groups for survivors of such abuse. If you feel physically threatened or injured, you can call 911. They help get out of this circle allow it.

Chapter Four

Narcissistic manipulation tactics

Gaslighting Narcissist

One of the What both fascinates and frightens narcissists is that it is difficult to understand what drives them, what their specific motives and goals are. We usually know that gaining the approval and acceptance of others is the main reason a narcissist lives, but what happens to the victim on a smaller scale? Sometimes narcissists think about a person's emotional health for fun or to see how far they can go - they think about illness and depression. But what else causes one person to treat another like that? We can get a little closer by looking at some basic aspects of the narcissist's personality. We have already discussed the general lack of empathy that is common to various types of narcissism. But there is another important aspect of Narcissus that she is trying to hide more than anything else, and that is insecurity. It is important to remember that narcissists are not born, personality is formed by various factors related to nature and nutrition that are too complex and unusual to function on a global scale. However, looking at the history of a narcissist, it can sometimes be suggested that some aspect of their education / childhood / adolescence may have contributed to their eventual narcissism. One of the most important reasons for determining why narcissism is such is that it is the lack of awareness and apparent purpose of using emotionally manipulative tactics such as suffocating the other person. What is gas light and how does it affect the victim over time? First of all, gas lighting is a manipulative process that over time leads the victim to question various aspects of their reality. To better understand what I mean, let's look at some warning signs that someone is biting.The biggest and most obvious sign is when a person tells a straightforward and shameless lie. They may look you in the face and tell you for sure it's not real, or they may be lying. The narcissist has good reason to believe in himself and this tactic, and may have used it before. He will lie to you until you think you know what is happening or not. People who are confident enough to lie like narcissists are more effective at letting them go. Their claims can be hard to prove because they seem so certain that what they are saying is true. Another warning sign is when narcissists start denying even what they said when they know they did it. If you feel the need to record the conversation at any time during sex, be careful, as this is a good sign that you are being bitten. A frivolous narcissist uses the things and people you value and turns them into emotional weapons against you. They can support their claims about you and your flaws through clever arguments and present them in a practical way that everyone but you probably knows. As they say, once they convince you that something is wrong with you, they will eventually absorb you and use other flaws or convince you to separate from other family members or friends. Separate yourself from your children. This can greatly annoy the victim of the bite, as the teacher's words often do not match the person's actions. He tells you things that lift your spirits and motivate you. But his behavior may contradict what he told you, you may find his words meaningless, and you may do something that disrespects him. For example, let's look at Claire. Maybe after a few conversations the narcissist, let's call him Mark, will notice that Clare is attracting him more and more. He carefully crafted his story and communicated exactly with those he wanted to see, even if it wasn't real. Let's say your relationship develops and you can convince him to do some things. Perhaps the fact that he is asking for a friend's opinion speaks volumes about his personality. Mark begins to sow insecurity, doubts and confusion about the things he appreciates. He can promise her the world and then she seems to disappear completely until he asks her to come back with him. So take this opportunity to find a weak point and tell him that he would be happier if he could improve his appearance, his work or something else. When he starts feeding himself lies and confusing things that contradict his behavior, gas lighting comes into play. Every time he tries to call her, she responds to him with more faith and conviction, telling him he was wrong. It is important to take small steps in this direction over time. It burns slowly, and before Claire realizes what is happening, she suddenly finds herself drowning in his confusion. I was convinced that the things Mark wanted to design for him would disappear and merge with reality. The trap is invisible and can last for years or even decades. A narcissist knows that the more they confuse you, the more they will rule you. They make you emotionally sensitive so that you feel he needs to guide you. Mark is able to take steps to turn Claire's closest friends against him and then blame them for all the emotional disorder she has experienced. oes of. At this point, Claire is psychologically addicted and feels she is nothing without Mark. The fall that broke the window and Narcissus 'victory sign makes you believe you're crazy, you don't know what you're talking about when you try to blame him for his lie or behavior. When they turn it off and finally listen to what's going on around you, they have complete control over you. They may stop joking and want to shoot you more, or they may get tired of hitting you and decide to accept a whole new challenge. When Claire finally realizes what they did to her, she may wonder why. What did he do with it? For those who suffer from narcissistic abuse, this is a problem that will likely need to be addressed. Ultimately, depending on how far the trauma has gone, the victim will have very low self-esteem and self-confidence because they have been emotionally beaten into feeling worthless and stupid. What is the answer to a serious question? Why meI love bombs and explosionsAnother manipulative tactic that narcissists love is the bombing and deflation. This cycle is mainly about showering the target with love, emotions, admiration, attention, gifts and anything else you think your target will appreciate. Dip her goal into anything that makes her feel good about creating some kind of addiction. He begins to associate her with the good feelings of receiving gifts, kindness, compliments, and everything else that bothers him, so he ties in with her sooner than expected. This allows the relationship to accelerate and move much faster than a healthy relationship. The exchange of "I love you" begins early and the victim falls in love with her when she falls into a romantic spiral. This is the embombado stage. Both bombs eventually fail, become exaggerated, and often become reasonable target expectations. Once the narcissist is convinced he has become a target, tactics change. Suddenly completely rejects. He decides to kick the pedestal he carefully placed on it and watch it try to turn. Suddenly, he is overwhelmed by shame, contempt, hatred and lack of love, and he is so attached to the narcissist that he wants to do anything to get it back. She will do everything necessary to get her back as best she can so that the embombing can resume. He wants you to be happy because he is happy when he is happy. He loses his presence and love. This gives the narcissist an abundance of narcissistic resources to enjoy and repeat the cycle. The cycle begins with romantic bombing and short-term devaluation, but slowly progresses to long-term devaluation and short-term devaluation and abuse until the relationship is in near final decline. At this point, the narcissist completely rejects the goal.Reflection and prediction-The reflex relates to the narcissist's tendency to wear a mask. I try to reflect my goals in myself, so to speak, seems more desirable. People tend to like people who are like them, and a narcissist knows this to some degree. Create an identity, create a mask to hide yourself from others, and that identity is constantly changing according to what others think. If you are lucky enough to attract the attention of a narcissist, you may have presented yourself exactly as you wanted. He likes what he likes, uses methods to build a relationship between you, and even if he doesn't know what he's talking about, he suddenly has the same goals as you. He is falsifying someone's interests Once she is interested, you can begin the stage of ambombo to further manipulate her. This behavior serves three different purposes for the narcissist. A narcissist has no real sense of self because he has never had one, and taking on someone else's character is a way to create a false identity. Imitation allows the narcissist to imitate someone who has what they want. If you imitate someone else's behavior, you are more likely to get the same results. Finally, copying others is as close as possible to logical empathy. The best thing you can do is build real relationships, not imitate someone else. Projection is reflexive, but it is reversed: the narcissist's attention is to the other person's thinking, while the narcissist thinks of others. Generally, this is done to show others their shortcomings and try to overcome their mistakes and mistakes. He often anticipates his guilt because they are too hard to control or because his guilt does not feed his frustration. He can describe his positive qualities, and if it fits the story, he will convince everyone. A more direct example of the pattern to observe usually appears when considering the relationship between a narcissistic parent and a child. Narges decides to create an ideal for his children or make a scapegoat. The idealized have become the golden children of narcissism, that is, they cannot do evil. Golden children are considered ideal and worthy, and Narcissus gives his achievements and glory. They are treated with the same respect that the narcissist thinks they deserve. Even if the golden child does something that seems problematic to others, the narcissist can still admire that behavior.On the other hand, the goat is the recipient of the negative side of the narcissist's personality. If the narcissist is not convinced that they are not smart, the victim will always be wise, even if they are in fact the best in their class at school. If a narcissist cares about ugliness, he will always care about the appearance of the scapegoat, even if the victim is conventionally attractive. Everything that is sacrificed is automatically considered inadequate and is often overlooked and minimized, diminishing any success. In both cases, Narcissus sees the Golden Boy and the

Goat as extensions: no one can be their people. Any attempt will be canceled as soon as possible. Play the victimAs briefly discussed above, Narcissus likes to play with his victim. This is a great tool for the narcissist to get what they want, and guilt is the easiest way to achieve that goal. He will try to get what he wants, and when he is denied that opportunity, he will turn everything back on to become a victim. Usually, a narcissist takes advantage of the other person's ability to show what they want, what the narcissist wants, making the other person feel guilty for having those feelings, usually making negative comments about you. ,FogAnother acronym, FOG, means Fear, Obligation and Guilt. Narcissists like to lose their victims in the fog in their relationships. When you try to drive along foggy roads and realize you can't do enough to drive safely, narcissists make sure you can't see enough to notice the red flags flying in your relationship fog. Too thick, vines disappear. In situations where you are afraid, you will do everything possible to avoid getting hurt. Ultimately, we are most afraid when there is a risk of injury or death. This is a way of saying that he is now in danger and must do everything he can to stay safe. Sometimes staying safe means listening to what the narcissist wants to protect. Duty pushes him to do the right thing for those he loves or to whom he is loyal. The benefit of narcissus When you love him, you feel a responsibility to care for him or to consider his feelings about things that affect us. You want to see him happy and healthy, and you want to do it out of love, and maybe he'll do for you something he can't buy. The narcissist uses this to his advantage and performs his duties whenever he seems to resist and feels guilty as a result. The narcissist is responsible for denying everything they want and feels guilty if they are more likely to give in. You can blame yourself for some adverse consequences, that means it's your fault if she gets hurt, or it's your fault if her kids get hurt because of your inaction. If he cheated on you, you can make him feel guilty by saying that he shouldn't feel him so alone and that he didn't realize the decision to concentrate on someone else. It is usually a last resort to keep you online because it takes a lot of energy to maintain and function. To have something that can control you, narcissists need to keep it online, which can be difficult in some areas of a relationship. Sometimes they seem to disappear, or threaten to be removed at will, or threaten to fire him if he disobeys. Although narcissists can avoid blame or consequences, they can benefit from the suffering of others. You can do this by blaming your mistakes on others, blaming others and creating confusion that hides their contribution.For example, imagine a man who made a big mistake. Is it part of a group of people? You can whisper that person A is guilty of B and point out all the ways that person B hurt them. You can point out that person B is trying to do his job according to the agreement and generally separate him from the other people and emphasize all the work he has to do now. A may decide to help B with his workload, believing he is ineffective. Nargis then approaches person B and says the same to person A. He complains that person A has overworked him due to the incompetence of person A and says that person A thinks he is better than everyone else. Others are beyond this simple task. Person B, who feels terrible around the narcissist, needs more than the narcissist's work, but is reluctant to help Person A. People A and B blame each other for all the trouble and extra work, not realizing that Il

Narcissus has thrown away more work on the m.lieDaffodils don't feel bad when gas-lit. They lie if they think this is the only way to get what they want. They have no problem telling people what they want to hear if they use it. Especially when he's trying to get someone back online, a narcissist may feel ready to make promises they don't want to keep to make sure the other person returns to complacency. For example, imagine a man who cheated on her husband. Narges may cry and apologize to her husband and promise not to do it again. She promises that she will get better and try to work independently, and her husband will later believe her. He believes her because most people are honest about what they do to correct the evil. When people are worried about something, they often do what they need to do to solve their problems. Narges says this just to please his target. He doesn't care about the pain she caused because he can't have much empathy. Instead, he makes a promise and fulfills his promise for a short time before going back to his old self for a while. This cycle continues over and over again with more and more rapid turns until the target becomes more or less normal and stops fighting it. .

Triangulation

The triangle represents deliberately creating conflict among others, while the narcissist manipulates the situation behind the scenes to get what they want. Form a triangle, whisper in the ears of others, tell conflicting stories, hoping to convince them that the problem is someone else's. This creates a conflict between the two people controlled by Narcissus, who completes the triangle. Two fightsHumiliatingA narcissist likes to secretly and openly humiliate others. By humiliating others, they can systematically and effectively destroy the self-esteem of others. That is why they can easily manipulate their chosen goals because their self-esteem is so damaged that it will be difficult for them to resist. Now, narcissists lack self-esteem. They feel better when they are surrounded by what they don't have. Narcissists can rely on being cruel and critical in naming, ignoring opinions, ignoring decisions, refusing congratulations, highlighting failures, or tearing down the other person. Later, she finally accepts it after repeatedly hearing that she cannot get a major job or promotion. Nargis 'words become the words he speaks to himself as he makes decisions and completes daily tasks. If narcissists have inserted negativity into you, that will be your default. For example, imagine a narcissist repeatedly telling you that you are not beautiful. Remember that you never do something right and it doesn't matter what it looks like. It can mean that you are lucky to be polite and lenient, or that you will always be single. She doesn't have a kitchen, she can't do her homework, she's under the middle age of people in a certain profession, her feet are too big, her clothes are too big, and your hair is the wrong color. This can give you some time to become too insecure to make a decision. After all, you were not wise enough or strong enough or ready to make those decisions and you came to that conclusion and trusted. The silent treatmentBecause all narcissists want attention and admiration more than anything else, they are afraid of being ignored more than anything else. According to Narges, the worst thing that can happen is not death or injury, but that everyone ignores and rejects what you are trying to do. In view of this, the narcissist believes that the most harmful and effective way to punish others is to ignore them. For some, this is a concern, especially if they have had a long-term relationship with the narcissist or if the narcissist is a parent or other close relative. The thought of this person being a mystic is terrible. You don't know why the narcissist did what they did, and they may refuse to talk to you for long periods of time, including days, weeks, months, or even years. Scare and intimidationAs expected, narcissists sometimes resort to threats or intimidation to keep people online. Because sometimes the only way to bully is to fear the consequences of his disobedience, and narcissists have no problem threatening or intimidating him. This could include threats to take the children away, ruin your reputation, sleep with your best friend, accuse her of beating or abusing her and physically threatening her if necessary. You may not even raise your hand to show that you are on the brink of physical violence using signs of aggression, such as throwing a glass at his head or knocking on a door. If he somehow managed to escape, I could take another step and engage him in battle. Often the line between illegal and annoying is different, and if he tries to emphasize it, he is said to be exaggerating it. Scare and threats are designed to make you feel that the best choice is to stay in the relationship without making waves and making a scene. onsequences.

Most of us Those of us who have studied this topic over time have noticed similarities in the types of narcissistic victims we choose. Narcissists know that strong, loving, self-assured people with clear, definite boundaries will not tolerate their disgust. That is why they are looking for people who have a weak sense of self, are socially responsible and generous, or are very willing to please others and treat them honestly and morally. They can choose victims who are deeply compassionate and therefore do not want to easily end even the most toxic relationships. Empaths are ideal candidates to be the next narcissist. Empaths are naturally programmed to fix difficult people and situations and generally improve things for everyone. Despite all the negativity and judgment about spirituality, angels, unicorns, and hippies they believe in, narcissists love nothing more than to wake up to the light that sees the best in the world, and Fighting Tigers can prove it. Everything is there. good spark So the typical empath looks at the narcissist and says, “Don’t worry, no matter what you do or say, I see God in you. I believe in you, one day you know you will do it, "Moderate nurses think" houses, lunch! "What Nazis want from Abaka is that they usually have many strengths, which they usually deliver, and again and again because or accept that everyone can be stationary. Selfishness, etc. In addition to self-help, another great lesson that empaths often have to learn through narcissistic disorder is to love and trust someone as much as we feel. Reiki, chanting and soul healing cannot cure everything, at least not in one life. Narcissists know they can lack empathy. All they have to do is talk in such a way that they hope for sympathy and perhaps the edge of spiritual awakening. If this plan is implemented, the empaths begin to believe, even though they have learned from past experiences, that all they want is love, proper attention, and rose quartz will finally come true. Narcissus of course laughs sarcastically because the importance of finding this wonderful book on shamanism leaves the room. The empath smiles happily and finally exhales, imagining the narcissist waiting with a sigh to enter the world of spiritual discovery, finding them in a row and forcing them to a meeting or a day of training. This is unexpected. I will mention it. They were filled with empathic psychic energy and bound by all sorts of contracts and dependencies that evoked compassion. They eat them all day and march victoriously to conquer the world. Remember, when we think of something, we send you energy, and hours after the narcissist leaves the building, empathy feeds on it, focusing on changing every nuance of the conversation in his mind, leaving behind the waves. It sends waves. Mental energy. A narcissist knows that after a narcissist becomes addicted to intense compassion, hot energy surrounds them throughout the day. Oh, I don't want to meet. Why don't you tell me when you're leaving so I can plan my time correctly? Why are you looking at all this at the last minute? I don't know if it works. I'm sure you haven't mentioned this before you . He may have remembered, but paid no attention. No, he certainly didn't mean that. If you didn't, why do you say you did? However, he was interested in the idea of redeeming the soul. Let's have a good discussion about it. Me too. Oh, what should I do now? I was suddenly very tired. I can't do much in two hours. This window is not big enough! Why is my time always interrupted? Why can't I do something else? Why can't you have a steady job? devil !! Why am I suddenly tired? Well, I know it's going to be hard today because it's your half day because everything you do is a bonus. Let's live with the day Why am I always so tired? This is ridiculous. I did nothing today. I wonder if she's interested in singing with me? whether he said or said Maybe that is changing. I don't know why now ???? I'm still going on the weekend. I need more time to think. It doesn't mean anything anymore, I'll go to sleep.

I need a nap, no, it's chocolate, I want chocolate. I lost count of how many times I passed this scene. Then, an hour and thirty minutes later, my phone rings and it's Edward calling to ask if I want something from the supermarket, good chocolate or fries. And Edward loved routine. I hated when things changed, even a little bit. He knew this because the change in routine was one of the things he was most indignant about. So I always tried to answer calls when I was expected. If I don't, it won't be a major problem, but he realizes and a few days later I try to call him about something unimportant and he doesn't answer. I always kept things. But I said yes to chocolate. I don't know how I survived the day without it. My life is full of small and friendly exercises. I didn't live in a golden cage, I lived in chocolate. Since it's not always available, I always want chocolate. Edward always knew what he wanted. Maybe because he's so good at creating need. That is why Narcissus rejoices in his infinite compassion, empathy, and his firm belief that everyone, cruel or destroyed, is worthy of love. A narcissist loves the praise that empathy feels and even thrives on the constant insecurity and frustration about everything that changes. They feel secure in the knowledge that empathy will never leave them, and their ability to maintain empathy as a reliable victim means that if they are intelligent, they can have energy reserves to live. Remember that when you think of a narcissist, you are sending them energy. No wonder the wind is easily crazy, because every crossover of the vibrant road, each stream changes, so we can trust part of a nursing feeling. The images and colds often used can be deep damage for all, but all things are deep, and when gifts and warm kisses they return to the first pump of addiction and may not believe. To focus. The problem is that these hugs are out of fashion, for some reason they don't go back into fashion, and neither Reiki readings nor angel cards will change that.3. Healthy and serious narcissismHealthy narcissismMost societies encourage positive traits such as self-confidence, charisma, or appreciation of genuine talents / traits that lead a person to believe that they are better than others without these traits. The ability to manage and motivate are equally positive qualities. These traits can be described as healthy narcissism. Many self-confident, extroverted and successful people have healthy narcissism and high levels of self-improvement, believe in themselves and seem limited by challenge and attention. But these positive aspirations do not include the belief that they are "better" than anyone else or the desire to do better. Faith and optimism are healthy, but overconfidence and belief in your positive qualities that make you better than others go from healthy narcissism to extremes. Confidence and self-esteem do not make healthy narcissists liked or manipulated. These health traits should not be confused with unhealthy or harmful narcissistic habits, as is often the case with many substances on the Internet. The 1% of people who scored the highest on healthy narcissism and the lowest on severe narcissism — people who light a room and inspire others to tear it down — agree with Dr. Malkin's findings. They see themselves and others through an optimistic lens and seek to inspire and motivate others rather than threaten them. success.

Narcissistic Victim, concentration and advantage. To some extent, positive feedback, concentration and satisfaction are a reward for good or benefit to be somehow. People with strong narcissism begin to keep well, protecting themselves to fall from above, as alcohol can prevent relaxation. In some people, unstable self-esteem leads to addiction. For everyone, love and praise cause pleasant feelings, and the brain releases the rewarding neurotransmitter dopamine. For people with low self-esteem and difficulty with dopamine regulation, this experience can be interesting. The pleasurable rush acts as a "tonic" to soothe deep painful emotions, creating negative feelings. When a person finds his talent, he can be successful, or dopamine is released if he or he or she finds a function or personality that gives them a positive reputation or attention (such as attractive, in exercise, learning) or to achieve the goals for the Most for most people, it is a way to develop health differences such as research and development of skills and interests. Many confident and kind people gain attention and importance and enjoy performing for others: comedians or talk shows like Ellen DeGeneres or James Corden. Probably, these people do not hide extreme narcissism. They will probably be polite, friendly and confident. For those who initially felt abandoned, bad, or "underestimated," the positive feelings gained through attention and recognition lead to the habit of constantly seeking similar experiences in an unhealthy way, subsisting on rites, nutrition, and this becomes kindness. attractive, successful or intelligent. This is called "narcissistic gratitude" and the word "proposal" is used as a drug. Not only that, after consuming or releasing large amounts of dopamine during narcissistic "development," some people experience "shock" in a similar but less intense way than drug addicts.As dopamine levels rise and fall, cocaine peaks and then decreases. This results in a rapid humor cycle and a constant search for additional supply to maintain standards. Additional effects of a sudden drop in dopamine include feelings of depression, anxiety, and irritability. This cyclical attitude does nothing to help the self-esteem of extreme narcissists, especially if they had low self-esteem before addiction. Guilt and shame can reinforce this cycle, causing the narcissist to swell and deny what is close to them and how they interact with the world as it separates. People who are high in extreme narcissism can become competitors because of the limited "bonuses" they receive from others. If you think of a person's concentration as a small package of "medicine," you can see how it works. The dose is low and the addict wants a lot for himself. Extreme narcissists usually feel threatened and jealous of those around them and act violently to maintain their sense of privilege and "goodness," "justice," or superiority. They can use various forms of manipulation to get as much narcissism as possible and justify it. Dopamine-releasing experiences such as alcohol, drugs, sex, or smoking are addictive. Dofamin's pleasant release and exaggerated self -esteem of the narcissist of course escapes from low dopamine or pain somehow defective or "bad". At the highest point of the spectrum, the constant requirement of control and service can reach an unresolved level, where the "offer" is insufficient to maintain an increased sense of self -claim of the nurses. Errors made by reviews or sensitivity of sensitivity can lead to an almost immediate and paralyzed return to low independent ownership. However, when we are in danger, our cognitive defenses are more effective in protecting us from such pain. The narcissist's defensive responses can intervene to prevent the threat and save the narcissist from confronting others who are responsible for his actions. For those in low levels of narcissism, this manifests itself as a very narcissistic part of the self that defends itself and does not take responsibility for its hurtful words and actions. They may resent any humiliation or threat to their self-esteem. However, for a human being, this choice between responsibility and safety can make the difference between swimming and efficiency. down.

Can extreme narcissists love?

The claim Narcissists "don't like" is a simple, negative aspect that does not analyze the technical features of what happens between high protection and narcissism. It forgets the idea of goodies and problems of people. It is an unrealistic black thought that not all mothers of narcissism can love their children or love their partner with a narcissistic life. People who have severe narcissism often feel good from "injury" to protect their breath from injuries and think too much without thinking about others, it depends on the excessive trend of narcissism, depending on the individual. Of course, they may be experiencing the same "enamored" response as the rest of us, releasing dopamine and "taking" and feeling that they are falling in love. Ironically, falling in love with a charming and adoring couple may seem like a pleasant experience, but it turns out to be selfish. Lovers try to satisfy their own emotional needs, not primarily to sympathize with their partners (recipients of unrequited love have been shown to be better able to understand the "love" part of a potential lover). If the romantic feelings of extreme narcissists resemble the experiences of healthy people, they can be discussed. If these feelings evolve into feelings of romantic love and affection comparable to those of youth, they are vague and vary from person to person.

Most low-level narcissists don't spend their time "filming" and are able to feel love and empathy in these moments. However, extreme narcissists are afraid to fall in love because they feel unworthy or incompetent. This can lead to fear of the pain and sensitivity that love brings when a partner leaves or betrays them. However, just because they are afraid of them, rejects them, or has little time to devote to them, does not mean they are insensitive. They may not be able to express it in a healthy way. If feeling vulnerable while in love makes them anxious, they may try to reduce that feeling through infidelity, reduce their partner, develop multiple attachments, reduce the strength of their primary attachment, or try to isolate themselves. Share the love in some way. When narcissistic reactions occur, love and affection for others cannot be prioritized. Before the feeling of love can appear or be expressed, one must first reduce the need to acquire material goods or protect oneself from threats to the ego. Where these activities are performed full-time, respect and compassion never show up. Protection against emotional pain is high on the brain's automatic priority list. Love is low in the list of automatic brain priorities. This does not mean that love is less welcome from our logical mind or our valuable organizations. This means that the mechanical responses of our brains (which are subconscious and unconscious) first move to protect us from emotional pain before considering higher concepts such as love and empathy. Learn more about real-life examples of showing love in a narcissistic relationship in Chapter 2. Extreme narcissists who abuse their loverThe higher the person, the more the narcissist sees other people as objects of his pleasure. They cannot be counted or loved, they can exist only to take what they can. They often pay only if it helps them get more. Some narcissists adore their loved ones and friends, suddenly see their flaws, devalue them, reject them without a second thought. Often they have a new lover or friend waiting to take care of them. If this has happened to you, you know how devastating and confusing it can be because narcissists are the center of your world and they don't seem to care that you are there. However, in some cases, they can stop lovers, friends and family members when necessary, pursue them and save them if they feel they are losing interest. Communication can be helpful because they may need sex or attention during their proposals are low.

Chapter Five

Narcissistic scale

Narcissism is This is not uncommon. This is a common trait found in humans, but only to varying degrees. The truth is that almost everyone has traits that indicate some narcissism. The concept of the spectrum comes from physics, and the frequency of narcissism indicates the severity of a person's condition. On the narcissistic spectrum, you will find that narcissists have a high sense of personal belonging and ego. However, the level of sensitivity and sense of grandeur are different. Psychologists often use this narcissism scale to test the level of narcissism and diagnose narcissistic personality disorder. The narcissism scale varies from 0 to 10. The smaller this number, the less narcissistic a person is. The higher this indicator, the more narcissistic a person is. Normal people usually have a healthy level of narcissism. Half of this spectrum includes those who are part of a healthy narcissism. They are realistic and have standard features. People with a higher frequency have more harmful elements. They have a sense of arrogance instead of healthy self-esteem. They are more aggressive than assertive and can give in. In large numbers, he will be selfish. They tend to have destructive behaviors and unhealthy thought processes. Therefore it must be concluded that at this level it is not very good or too little. The best position in the spectrum is in the middle. Let's look at different numbers in terms of size and meaning:A score of 0 on the scale indicates a very low level of narcissism.

A person who is set to 0 is usually very generous and easily manipulated by others. They care more about others than about their own needs and easily give in to others. These people are terrible and humble. However, they lack a sense of self-worth and self-respect. There are people who are at level 1 on the spectrum slightly higher than 0. They tend to focus a little more on their personal needs. However, these people do not trust secular meetings and usually avoid communication. They are easily overworked and therefore timid. They are also modest, but respectful. Levels 2 and 3 have more social units. These people can have dreams and goals. They feel more comfortable in social situations than level 0 or 1. However, they often do not like to draw attention to themselves. Sometimes they can get out of their comfort zone, but usually they close. Levels 4, 5 and 6 include individuals identified as healthy narcissists. These people are modest, but have high self-confidence. They love and appreciate the attention of others. They know when they deserve recognition and when to let others get the attention. They don't have a sick need to be the center of everything. They do not go so low in the spectrum to avoid observation. They are equally humble and modest. Levels 7 and 8 are a little more narcissistic than healthy. They like to show their results and things. However, they realize that they are wrong and are trying to get better. But these people tend to oscillate between good and bad behavior. They love attention and are not completely constant personalities. Level 9 includes people who develop awareness and knowledge. They always try to be at the center of everything. However, sometimes they realize their unrealistic need for attention and appreciation. That makes them guilty, but they are still trying to hide their guilt. They know that constant attention to them is terrible, but they can't resist. Level 10 is at the end of the spectrum. This includes the most selfish and arrogant people. Such people have a high opinion of themselves and are classified as NPD. They are known to do anything to get what they want. They lie, cheat, steal and do anything to get attention. They like to show superiority and make others feel inferior. There are three types of daffodils that are harmful to health. Their characters are different, but they are all harmful narcissists. The characteristic of these three kinds of people is that they consider themselves more and better than others. Extroverted Narcissists: Loud and disgusting people who crave attention. They are very friendly and like to be in social situations. They live in any society to attract attention. They always post pictures on social media and want to present their durability and expensive purchase. When they achieve something, they are praised until a kingdom comes. Introverted narcissists: Fear of being judged by others and possibly avoiding it. They think they're better than others, but they don't want others to know it. They like to communicate and are comforted by a sense of superiority. Urban skiers: These are people who want to show others what they can do in the shortest possible It is time to ask for nothing in return, they want others to know that they are saviors of people and always give more than they receive. Now you see how different narcissists can be. You can observe yourself and those around you to see where they fall on the narcissistic spectrum. This will help you get to know your personality better and deal with it better.

Chapter Six

How to tell if you're trapped in a network of narcissists

In most In some cases, people do not know that they are suffering from narcissism. They confuse what they see in a relationship as a normal part of any couple. Even when abuse is rampant, people live in denial that their wife is a narcissist. The main reason for this is their excessive flattery and praise during the idealization stage. A narcissist knows how to just start a relationship and attract a patient to himself so that the first few days are romantic. Victims are lost and want to get back with their partners at this point, so they do everything they can. They are so dependent on the hope that the relationship will get better that they don't even know when they are being abused. Below are some signs that you may be caught by a narcissist. Frequent threatsMost narcissists threaten their victims with things they don't want. In response, when the victim is threatened, she tends to humiliate herself, which gives the narcissist more opportunities to control her. If your partner continues to threaten to leave, you won't get what you owe if they don't get it, and you're probably dealing with a narcissist. They use this approach because it is most effective when it creates fear, doubt and guilt. Your partner threatens to show that you are not comfortable in the relationship. Because they create risks, you avoid creating problems because you are afraid they will work. For example, if they threaten to leave you and you don’t need them, it will be hard for you to leave because you know they are not begging you to stay.You don't feel yourselfIf you feel you have no goals or aspirations, you have given up. At this point in his life, because of the person with whom he is in a relationship, he has set aside his basic desires and needs and sacrificed his emotional well-being for the pleasure of the abuser. Once in his life he can be full of life. He is driven by dreams and goals. But now she feels alive to fulfill the goals and needs of her lover. You’ve reached a point where your life revolves around them and you have nothing but the relationship. This means that you have forever sacrificed your rights and satisfied the violator. Healthy relationships do not mean giving up personal security, friendships, hobbies and goals, but rather lead to reaching their full potential and living a happy life. In addition to the sacrifices, you will later realize that you cannot satisfy your partner and the sacrifices will be wasted.You have health problemsMost people in narcissistic relationships live in denial and do everything they can to hide the difficulties and problems they face. When they are severely affected, they try to maintain a good image in society. If you find yourself in this situation, you have fallen into the trap of narcissism. Some people develop serious health problems that they did not have before the relationship began. You can get older compared to most of your peers, which is called premature aging. The stress, anxiety, and depression you experience in a chronically violent relationship can suppress your immune system. At this stage, it means that you are prone to various physical and mental illnesses and diseases. Also, if you have nightmares or insomnia, it is because you are traumatized by the visual memories. People in healthy relationships don’t feel this way. Isolated personOne of the ways narcissists use to ensure complete control over you is to isolate them from loved ones. If they know that your parents or friends can help you understand that you are a victim of abuse, they will try to separate you from them. Some narcissists use a slanderous campaign to label you as someone with a personality disorder. Friends will no longer trust you and others will deliberately avoid you. In other cases, you isolate yourself from your friends because you are ashamed of the abuse you are experiencing. If so, then you want to laugh with your friends. It is important to understand that by doing this you are empowering the criminal. However, due to guilt and lack of understanding of psychological abuse, people follow him until he makes a mistake. According to Bergman and others, misperceptions of others, including family and friends, can undermine the belief that narcissists are violent. (2011) in their analysis revealed how narcissists use their manipulation techniques. So, because you are afraid that no one will understand you, you withdraw from society instead of seeking help, avoiding revenge or temptation. If you find yourself in this situation, you need to reconsider your position because you are stuck in a sick position. relationship.

If you blame yourself

For abuse, The actions of narcissists are really inhuman, but they don't realize it and want to do it to others. They usually use something called reverse psychology. Relationships work best in the idealization stage. They do kind, gentle and gentle things to win their hearts and love. In the following stages, they change in every way and become aggressive. They act both cold and hot, confusing him as to who they are. Most victims do this without realizing that their partners are doing it on purpose. A narcissist excels at creating love triangles in which he involves another person, whether it is a stranger or an ex-lover, to intimidate his victim. In this case, the victim tends to internalize the fear of not being good enough, and this leads to competition for the abuser's approval and attention. Also, if you are comparing yourself to others in healthy and happy relationships, consider why your partner treats others with respect. Of course, "Why me?" You such questions lead to guilt. The truth is, you shouldn't blame yourself. A criminal is an aggressor because you have no doubt that they caught you in cyberspace.If you are afraidWith narcissists in prosperous relationships, do what you want to achieve more success or deprive your victims of their freedom. In this regard, they should approve or comment on what their lovers are doing. If you're in a relationship where you have to ask your partner for permission to do certain things, you don't have freedom. If you feel that this is becoming a threat to your partner, then it is time to leave the relationship. Narcissus teaches you to combine fields of success, talent, enthusiasm and happiness with ruthless and ruthless behavior. Therefore, you should fear success more than your partners will accept because you will be blamed or rebuffed against you. The conditioning made him feel desperate, anxious, depressed, and most importantly, to hide his abilities. It is important to understand that the reason the criminal is limited in what you want to achieve is because he knows that if you succeed, he will lose control over you.If you feel isolatedWhen you are physically and mentally disconnected from your identity, consciousness, emotions, and memory, you fall into a narcissistic web. Experts consider dissociation as the essence of trauma. In this situation, a person separates himself from feelings, thoughts, images, sounds and physical emotions to manage his life. If you still feel emotionally uncomfortable after a traumatic event, this is not normal. If repression, addictions, obsessions, and disabilities have become your lifestyle to help you escape abuse, your partner is a narcissist. It's not normal, but your brain has developed ways to block the effects of pain so you don't have to deal with scary situations. If this happens, you will be disconnected from loved ones, criminals, your environment and yourself. At this point, you need to find a trauma specialist. They will help assess your status after enrollment items.

You can't Expect silence when you meet a real narcissist, someone with a narcissistic personality disorder. You will have an inner experience of feeling a mixture of disgust, helplessness, surprise, anger, and depending on what is happening, disappointment or shame. You will explore these feelings deeply. There are many times when you realize that you have been attacked by a narcissist. Some people hate that person and start hating that feeling. Unfortunately, emotions still appear. This friend is the most helpful and friendly person I have ever met, but his narcissism permeates caution and kindness like a knife. What if you meet a man who is unsympathetic, constantly in need of praise, arrogant, ostentatious, blames you for everything, and always has the audacity to brag about himself? How do you take care of yourself when you meet such a person? One of the best ways to deal with someone when you have such strong feelings is to face the situation and talk about it with the person who is hurting you. It's the best way to do things, but narcissists never care about how you feel. Most arguments with narcissists do not help their resentment, helplessness, or anger. Worse, they fight with the narcissist, who can miscarry. There was a time when I had to deal with a narcissist and this person was the person he cared about. I wrote the script for hours and carefully considered it. I shared with them what I was feeling and also understood what this person was feeling and what might be going on in their head. I got only anger and guilt. When I tried to confront this person and tell them how I felt, the reaction surprised me. So how do you talk to a narcissist? Let us consider the following points:Always look at the bigger pictureYou have to remember to look at the bigger picture. You cannot change or control another person, but you can change how that person governs or influences you. Always ask yourself what is important in any situation. Narcissists know how to catch you and swallow you completely. Their stories and thoughts will continue to fascinate you and you need to notice that sooner and see the bigger picture. This human is just one of the 8 billion people on this planet. So why would you let someone have so much power over your emotions? Always look at your strengthsFirst, you should try to identify the traits that are your strongest. That's why you need to use these features intensively. Sit still and write down your five strengths. When dealing with narcissists, pay attention to these traits and stay calm. Always use your strength to stay healthy.Avoid toxicityIt's hard to deal with a person who has a hard time living well. That way you can completely avoid the situation that leads to a lot of problems. For example, if you avoid a situation that causes anxiety, the anxiety may increase. In case of poisoning, avoid contact with vapors, as vapors can cause nettles. You should always consider your personality as your strong point. This can help with emotional regulation, so it's easier to control your impulses when you're around a narcissist. You should always use your powers to waste time due to non-toxic effects. Use a narcissistYou should always ask yourself what traits or behaviors a narcissist exhibits or is harmful. You need to spend some time to understand what is bothering you. Is it because they underestimate their goodness or justice? Do you pretend to be spiritual? Are they human? Often the most important forces for you are the ones you underestimate or overestimate. These preferences are called keyboard shortcuts. If someone doesn't show you this power, he feels crazy. Knowing which switches are important to you will increase your self-awareness. Thus, you can use this knowledge to your advantage when dealing with conflicts or problems. Always be very sensitive to the behavior of others. When dealing with a person who is narcissistic but does not have a narcissistic personality disorder, it is good to understand that person's behavior. You need to take the time to try to understand the person's strengths and assess the strengths they are above or below usage. This helps maintain the goal of seeing their own characteristics. If a person with a narcissistic personality disorder exhibits unhealthy behaviors that affect their knowledge. It is difficult for such people to identify forces that are being abused or underused. If a person is not kind to others, they cannot feel that they are not using social intelligence or kindness.Like wise, transient quality and the need to evaluate it cannot be regarded as unfit for use. Such behavior requires a completely different explanation.

This is because these people are abusing their power. He needs to find out if the narcissist is using the resistance of his personality to harm or manipulate others. Research shows that people often use persistence and creativity for harmful purposes. These people can use other personality forces to strengthen or humiliate another person. You should choose one of the strategies mentioned in this section start taking care of yourself. Narcissus won't worry about it, but you can do it.

Sometimes it is easy To say that someone is a narcissist is sometimes impossible. Manifestations of narcissism differ from person to person. As we mentioned before, there are six types of narcissism, each different from the other. Sloths, addicts, predators and psychopaths are easily identifiable. All three types of narcissists expose their narcissistic behavior openly. They are not afraid to express their feelings and do not refrain from actions. Violent narcissists can be confused with ordinary criminals.On the other hand, hidden narcissists and seducers are impossible to detect. They are very secretive and carry out their plans calculatedly. One of the most important factors in identifying narcissists is the similarity of their motivations. Although some may seem friendly, the ultimate goal of a narcissist is domination .All narcissists think they are superior and will use any means to gain dominance. Even those who use charms show the first signs of their ultimate intentions. From the beginning, the narcissist tries to control his thoughts and mind. Narcissists tend to control the people they want to control and target those they perceive as most vulnerable. Narcissism manifests itself in two main ways: emotional reaction and conscious behavior. Emotional response refers to how a person reacts in certain emotional situations. Narcissistic behavior is more likely to manifest when a person is angry or sad. When narcissists are upset, they are verbally, emotionally, sexually or physically violent.What a person does when it is angry or sad plays an important role in defining their personality. Conscious reaction refers to the actions and decisions that a person makes in his mind. Examining a person's daily actions, words, and deeds can help diagnose narcissism. Narcissists often show anger and resentment even when they are not being bullied. In everyday activities, narcissists are perfectionists. They usually associate daily activities with successful people they admire. Their words are self-righteous, and they are quick to make friends with those who admire them and reject those who criticize them. It is impossible to recognize a narcissist if you do not pay attention to what surrounds you. The ability to recognize narcissism begins with self-awareness. Before you can understand the actions and feelings of the narcissist, you need to be able to recognize your own feelings. The ability to understand and manage the emotions of others is called emotional intelligence (EQ). In psychology, we talk about people with a high EQ who can read other people's emotions and manage them. People with high EQ are not easily manipulated. Narcissists exploit those who lack emotional intelligence. People with low EQ are easy to handle. Their ideological principles can influence them and they are often seen following others. Let's move on to the concept of emotional intelligence and its impact on interpersonal relationships. That said, narcissism can be easily detected if you are curious and paying attention to everything around you. You can identify narcissism by observing a person's daily activities, paying attention to their visions and dreams, observing their perceptions of others, and observing their reactions to emotional problems. Five ways to recognize a narcissistNarcissists are very responsive to criticism and oppositionAs mentioned before, narcissists are vulnerable to people. They react explosively to problems that others do not. If you notice that someone is resisting criticism, correction or anything negative, you should start paying attention to their actions. It is true that some people appreciate negative reviews. However, while most people don't like negative reactions, a narcissist's response can be explosive in addition to resistance. Narcissists believe they are superior and do not accept opinions or suggestions that say otherwise. When a narcissist is asked to reveal their weaknesses, they rush to lie to protect themselves from showing them off.

This behavior of narcissistic people is described as a narcissistic dilemma. This is because narcissists are often confused about whether to show their true self and confess their weaknesses, or to use false persons and never confess their flaws. It is believed that the main reason most narcissists are so defensive is that they are afraid and don't want others to see them. Narcissists have low self-esteem about what they want to create world.

Show low self-esteem

If you're Not emotionally intelligent, you will never see low self-esteem among narcissists. They try to hide their self-esteem with an exaggerated personality. Narcissists are proud to be weak in all walks of life. You will see a man who has no wealth and is connected with the rich of the world. For them, they are ashamed to shrink.

They don't want to be associated with poverty, so they think they have money and hide it. They associate everything they have with wealth and class. They want to buy only high quality products and do not believe that others can have a more valuable product than them. All of these factors are a sign of low self-esteem. In a relationship, they can become aggressive and accuse the other party of infidelity without evidence. Most narcissistic partners only become aggressive out of paranoia, not because they have been betrayed. If a narcissist believes that someone is worthy of a life partner, they threaten and try to instill fear in them. A narcissist is afraid of loneliness. A narcissist uses anxiety, bullying and mockery to hide his low self-esteem. Even if they never confess that they have low self-esteem, they can confide in a friend or loved one. Most narcissists have an inner personality that they try to hide.

Some narcissists develop a narcissistic personality due to traumatic events in childhood. They remain in the child's psyche for a long time and protect his personality from discovery. They are usually afraid to face their childish fears and let go of what holds them back. You have to be very careful to recognize the weakness and low self-esteem of a narcissist. You have to be careful with every word you say and everything you do. From time to time they give conditions for repentance and repentance. Narcissists are very honest and protectiveNarcissists have an endless need to defend their actions. People who do unfortunate deeds still find a way to protect themselves. Narcissists are not criticized for this betrayal. They are arrogant, exaggerated, stubborn and defensive. Every word that comes out of their mouth is defense. Although they are part of a group, they tend to distinguish themselves from group bugs. But they are quick to celebrate the team's success. Narcissists dislike group work because they believe that group members do not meet the standards they have set in their minds. When they work in a team, they control and then lead to discord in the team. Narcissists are only friends with those who follow or fear them. They don't make friends with people who question their way of thinking. Even if the facts do not match, they must be true.Interestingly, they pay a lot of attention to everything they do and make sure everything is done correctly. When they fail, they remove their anger against everyone. At work, they are quick to blame other employees for their mistakes. According to him, there are no words to apologize for. They don't even use the word sorry when they know they did something wrong. He gets nervous easilyThe most obvious sign of narcissism is the narcissist's reaction to the words, thoughts, and actions of others. Narcissists are very sensitive because of their subtle personality. They get angry because of problems that others can't tell anyone. His anger is largely triggered by words or actions that seem to contradict his ideologies. However, this type of reaction also occurs in people with other personality disorders. For example, borderline people and very sensitive people show anger when questioned. For Narcissist, their passion stems from the fact that challenges can weaken them or prevent them from achieving their goals. In this case, most narcissists try to hide their weaknesses and control them. For example, if a narcissistic person is interested in a sexual partner, it is easy to attribute the narcissistic personality by dismissing his or her circumstances. Even charismatic narcissists are still prone to anger. The best way to recognize attractive narcissists is to constantly thwart their attempts. Seductive narcissists are usually patient. However, over time, they become impatient and begin to show anger. Any action that makes him seem weak or incompetent will cause outrage. Angry narcissists are physically or emotionally aggressive. They start with threats and then become aggressive .

Narcissists design traits, traits, and personalities that they do not take into account

In most casesNarcissists show aspects that are not part of their theme. Because they believe that if they keep saying they are kind or kind, they are hiding their true self from people. Most narcissists do not recognize their true nature. They will work with charismatic leaders and other successful people. His true identity lies within. If you're curious, you'll soon find out that they don't like what they're saying. In short, the characters they choose serve to devalue and discredit others. They report mistakes by focusing on the shortcomings of other people so that no one can concentrate on them. They believe they are great if they highlight the weaknesses of other people. Narcissists are quick to judge and find a way to show the terrible in others. Thus, they direct all negative energy towards other people and try to protect their personality.It is not possible to understand the personality of a narcissist if you are indifferent. They hide their true identity well. Sometimes they can use manipulation and in some cases force. You cannot accept it under any circumstances. Most narcissism begins with mental manipulation. If they find that they can easily fall under their spell, they hide their other symptoms. However, if their emotional intelligence is greater than they think, they resort to physical violence. You have to be careful to protect yourself from any narcissistic abuse. If you allow narcissism for a long time, you will eventually be brainwashed and lose the ability to make good decisions. Victims of narcissistic abuse need years to recover, and some never recover. It is your duty to protect yourself from such people. Read the signs in advance and separate yourself from your thoughts.The secret language of narcissists, psychopaths and sociopaths. The only way to protect yourself from narcissism is to understand their language. According to statistics, 1 in 25 people in the United States is UU. You have symptoms of narcissism, psychopathy or sociopathy. Narcissists, psychopaths and psychopaths all share a secret language. We will consider each of these diseases below. One of the outward aspects of narcissism is selfishness. They share this role with sociologists and psychiatrists. According to Dr. Martha Stout of

Harvard Medical School, people with NPD speak the language of madness, with words like lettuce, pathological jealousy, and gas light. The style of narcissism follows the cycle of narcissism, which we will explore later. Reading and understanding the cycle of narcissism is essential to discovering its beauty. Initially, some narcissists are attractive and alluring. You may not be able to tell a narcissist if you know him because he is wearing a mask. First, they can be beautiful, fun and very romantic. They can inspire you right and lead you to success in any field. Some narcissists seem very harmless and become close when they become friends. They gain your trust and convince you that they care about your interests. In the first stage of the cycle, anyone can fall into the trap. However some points should give you a signal. If you feel that someone is using your success to glorify you, retire. Narcissus can make him win so they can be considered victorious. In some cases, they help charities to appear friendly. Narcissists always hide personal motives in their actions. Be careful if you find someone to associate your success with yours. Such people are also very authoritative. Even if someone calls you a narcissistic "me or me," they try to present you as possessive. Psychiatrists and psychiatrists have chronic language manipulation. As narcissists, psychopaths and sociopaths, they must first outdo their victims. They use brainwashing and manipulation techniques to lure people into their network. Some use their abuse to brainwash and evaluate a person. Narcissists and sociopaths use emotional abuse to devalue a person. They make sure the victim is helpless and ready to follow their instructions without question. People with narcissism usually experience anxiety, fear, and helplessness, sometimes experiencing suicidal thoughts. In most cases, the narcissist seeks to make the victim an object. They contact anyone who mentions the toy to check their satisfaction. The authors point to emotional power as the main reason why it is dangerous to use narcissism. In human psychology, the brain circuit of physical and emotional pain is the same. In other words, if it causes physical pain, a slap in the face or the use of hurtful words, it can have the same effect on the brain. A person who is verbally abused on a daily basis can suffer serious emotional damage and have trouble recovering in the long run. Emotional scars are difficult to remove, and most narcissistic victims have PTSD or severe PTSD.Psychiatry and Sociology Learning the language of narcissism helps protect against its forms. An important factor to understand Cruelty among narcissists is not overt, but hidden. His actions and desire to cause pain are deeply rooted in his works. Everything they do, from facial expressions to gestures, sounds and words, often does not match their actions. His cruelty is purposeful, and his actions are unrepentant. In most cases, repentance and repentance are part of the victim's online language. Narcissistic language has many verbal devices. All communication tools are designed to cause pain and silence when necessary. Their goal is to weaken the victim's self-esteem and increase narcissism. In their arsenal, they use such cruel means as sarcasm, insults, a shift in feelings of guilt, a sadistic tone and silence. Narcissists are friendly when they see their world well. Any attempt to undermine your comfort will cause negativity in your personality. Here are some tips to help you understand the language of psychiatrists, sociopaths, and narcissists:without mercyIf you find yourself working with or dating someone, you should proceed with caution. First, they can be sympathetic and kind. However, it matters how they treat others. See if the person shows the same compassion for family members as siblings, mother, or father. The way a person treats other family members shows their true character. Most narcissists never introduce their partner to family or friends. If you're in a relationship with someone who doesn't consider you friends or family, start reading the red flags. The proximity of the household will emphasize the true essence of man. A bad boy can easily pretend to be with you, but will quickly explode in front of his brother. Most narcissists do not have good relationships with other family members.Beware of selfishnessEgo is the language that governs the life of a narcissist. In the early stages, they can pretend to give you everything you want. The best way to tell if they are selfish or trapped is to see how they treat others. His actions towards others reflect his true character. When a person is in love or obsessed with someone, they can exhibit the desired behavior. However, the drugs are slowly disappearing and true nature is beginning to permeate us.Hidden rolesNarcissists care and control. The first key to understanding language is to find your true self. Narcissists quickly become defensive when you try to ask personal questions and look for evidence - narcissists thrive on lies. Click to find out the truth about your past, previous relationships, family life and more. A narcissist must ask these questions before he can fully control his mind. Why are we attracted to narcissists?Victims of narcissistic abuse often suffer from post-traumatic stress disorder or narcissistic abuse syndrome. A big mystery for many clinicians is how far-reaching the effects of narcissistic bullying can be. However, an obvious factor is that victims always blame themselves. A victim of narcissistic abuse is not a criminal. In most cases, the victims are innocent and easily trust the people they come in contact with. Sufferers usually do not see evil in people, but believe in the good intentions of all. Dead, victims of narcissists, people who have accepted a free life and have no obstacles. They are carefree and don't care much about what the world says. They are ready to enjoy life and have fun. They take risks and are willing to offer love, even if the changes are not great.No one is attracted to narcissists. This is a narcissist who sees a person as a victim. Just because a narcissist attacks you doesn't mean you're weak. A narcissist sees a man as a relative. A narcissist is looking for weak and defenseless victims. However, narcissists can deal with any situation. The strategy they adopt can leave everyone behind. The narcissist's first step is to remove the target victim from friends and family. They make sure that their victims have no one to turn to for help in life. When they get a victim there, they start harassing. There are three main reasons why a narcissist is attracted to a particular person. For selfishnessNarcissists like to show their superiority over others. They want to show that they are great and deserve better in life. When a narcissist sees someone who can help them reach this state, they are attracted to them. You can find a friend who is just your friend because it increases your social status. Narcissists are looking for people to lift them. Unfortunately, when they become friends with the person they love, they try to keep the relationship going by being violent. Narcissists are attracted to the most beautiful woman or the most attractive man. They capture the victim. When a person enters her claws, she tries Close them with insults, intimidation and threats. Narcissists cannot maintain relationships because their true selves are hidden. The initial complaint is later dismissed and replaced by manipulation to maintain the relationship. The ultimate goal of the narcissist is to ensure that the manipulator does not leave. Their goal is to continue to benefit from the sacrifices they make in their lives. If they do not maintain these relationships with reasonable social norms, they begin to abuse. Narcissists are attracted to people they perceive as weakIf the narcissist sees him weak, he may try to use him to advance his ambitions. Narcissists prey on vulnerable people for pain and pleasure. They also invite vulnerable people as personal fans. Narcissists want people to admire them and speak well of them in public. They show someone who can become a doll of selfishness.Narcissists target people for financial gainNarcissists can tell people they want something. They can affect a person through manipulation or intimidation. They try to get money or property from someone without using force, but can end up being aggressive. Narcissus doesn't care if you're poor or not. They financially drain someone to the last penny and then dump the victim. In many cases, such people use love to capture their victims. They are looking for people who are serious about love and can concentrate on them. Narcissists are attracted to highly skilled peopleNarcissists are usually obsessed with fame, money and titles. They may refer to a person who occupies such a high position to advance their intentions. They want someone they can work with to improve their position. In some cases, the goal may be material gain or pleasure. A narcissist has sex with someone he knows to show himself worthy of high society status.

Chapter Seven

Narcissism in the families of the Family

There, we Learn to see yourself and the world as good habits like cleanliness and hard work. And where we follow corruption, sometimes, depending on our progress, it's very bad. Some mental disorders are a direct result of our education. Things like antisocial personality disorder, borderline personality disorder and narcissistic personality disorder are rooted in childhood abuse and neglect and have lasting effects in adulthood. Sometimes these problems are detected by particularly experienced parents or teachers.

Sometimes no one notices this because they don't know what to look for. In this chapter, we look at narcissism in families, studying narcissistic parents, narcissistic children, and siblings.Meet MargaritaDaisy is a beautiful thirty-four year old woman with a good job, a pleasant part of life and an active social life. He lost weight from his college, but he doesn't do much, but it's not enough for someone who calls him "fat." Recently, she lives in one widow's mother, and she helps her homework and children's job on the weekend. As Daisy approaches, he sees the trophies that have won Ellen's oldest sister, and she is now married and lives all over the country. An entire library is dedicated to Ellen's memories of the childhood competitions she won during her college sports days. Amma was a sports coach and loved cheering her team on, speaking at awards ceremonies and giving interviews to the local newspaper. So she put Ellen through all these activities and saw the results for her daughter herself. Ellen wanted to concentrate on her mother, and in time she left to make sure she had her. He began to subtly and openly mock Daisy. He would comment on Daisy's hair or clothes or call her "ugly" and "stupid" in high school, push her away from home as long as possible, and participate in any club or university activity. To his mother's horror and his sister's amusement, he began to weigh himself. Then he entered a good public university, set up the traditional Freshman Top 10, and gained an additional thirty pounds before graduation. He worked hard in his lectures, made the list of principals and completed the Summa Come Lat Niti. Although her father praised her academic qualifications and awards, Daisy's mother and sister reacted well enough to see her do well, but they showed no interest or pride in Ellen's success. Overestimating Daisy's weight, her mother called her "fat" and "shaky," holding Ellen's athletic physique as the norm. His older sister teased him and called him fat. When Daisy reached adulthood, she completely abandoned the lives of her mother and sister. They met for the first time a few days after the death of their father in memory of their father. Now a mother and a successful fitness teacher, Ellen is kind to her sister, but Daisy recognizes the smiles and furrows her eyebrows under her face. Mom looks at her and says she's glad Daisy finally showed up, though she overheard her mom and sister comment on her weight later in the afternoon. After her father's death, Daisy begins to feel the pressure to do small things for her mother. It did not involve excuses or pleas for a better relationship, but a heartfelt insistence from her mother and sister that Daisy was responsible. "At least you can take care of him," Ellen said. Her relatives called her mom in her eyes and never acknowledged that Daisy's childhood was as beautiful as her sister's and wanted to know why she didn't spend time with her mom. They said: "He is alone now. It was a long time ago and I hope it wasn't too bad. ' It was customary for Daisy to finally break up, but soon regretted it. When she goes to her mother, she has such a conflict: she brags to Ellen how beautiful she is, how carefree she is, where she goes this summer or on vacation with her husband. As he is smart that he did in the competition, his daughter Taylor follows his stairs when he started sports and athletics. It affects Daisy's weight and face, the mother gladly said "You are sure you can't worry about yourself" because it criticizes how to find a man to find a better man to support him. He is very stable, he slipped into phone calls, and sometimes emails, so Daisy felt a child: anger, tired, depression. Narcissistic parentsDaisy's story - the adult son of an evil narcissist. In her most basic form, her mother saw her children as reflections of herself, not as separate individuals. As a result, a very clear girl, married to a rich man and now gains all glory and exacerbates you for the reach of race and race, which is now a jet. She grew up as her daughter. Single Margoraid is one of the academic achievements that did not understand or understand or did not understand, and are in close relationships with peaceful education with the mother who raped her. Learn to see yourself and the world as good habits like cleanliness and hard work. And where we follow corruption, sometimes, depending on our progress, it's very bad. Some mental disorders are a direct result of our education. Things like antisocial personality disorder, borderline personality disorder and narcissistic personality disorder are rooted in childhood abuse and neglect and have lasting effects in adulthood. Sometimes these problems are detected by particularly experienced parents or teachers. Sometimes no one notices this because they don't know what to look for. In this chapter, we look at narcissism in families, studying narcissistic parents, narcissistic children, and siblings.Meet MargaritaDaisy is a beautiful thirty-four year old woman with a good job, a pleasant part of life and an active social life. He lost weight from his college, but he doesn't do much, but it's not enough for someone who calls him "fat." Recently, she lives in one widow's mother, and she helps her homework and children's job on the weekend. As Daisy approaches, he sees the trophies that have won Ellen's oldest sister, and she is now married and lives all over the country. An entire library is dedicated to Ellen's memories of the childhood competitions she won during her college sports days. Amma was a sports coach and loved cheering her team on, speaking at awards ceremonies and giving interviews to the local newspaper. So she put Ellen through all these activities and saw the results for her daughter herself. Ellen wanted to concentrate on her mother, and in time she left to make sure she had her. He began to subtly and openly mock Daisy. He would comment on Daisy’s hair or clothes or call her “ugly” and “stupid” in high school, push her away from home as long as possible, and participate in any club or university activity. To his mother's horror and his sister's amusement, he began to weigh himself. Then he entered a good public university, set up the traditional Freshman Top 10, and gained an additional thirty pounds before graduation. He worked hard in his lectures, made the list of principals and completed the Summa Come Lat Niti. Although her father praised her academic qualifications and awards, Daisy's mother and sister reacted well enough to see her do well, but they showed no interest or pride in Ellen's success. Overestimating Daisy's weight, her mother called her "fat" and "shaky," holding Ellen's athletic physique as the norm. His older sister teased him and called him fat. When Daisy reached adulthood, she completely abandoned the lives of her mother and sister. They met for the first time a few days after the death of their father in memory of their father. Now a mother and a successful fitness teacher, Ellen is kind to her sister, but Daisy recognizes the smiles and furrows her eyebrows under her face. Mom looks at her and says she's glad Daisy finally showed up, though she overheard her mom and sister comment on her weight later in the afternoon. After her father's death, Daisy begins to feel the pressure to do small things for her mother. It did not involve excuses or pleas for a better relationship, but a heartfelt insistence from her mother and sister that Daisy was responsible. "At least you can take care of him," Ellen said. Her relatives called her mom in her eyes and never acknowledged that Daisy's childhood was as beautiful as her sister's and wanted to know why she didn't spend time with her mom. They said: "He is alone now. It was a long time ago and I hope it wasn't too bad. ' It was customary for Daisy to finally break up, but soon regretted it. When she goes to her mother, she has such a conflict: she brags to Ellen how beautiful she is, how carefree she is, where she goes this summer or on vacation with her husband. As he is smart that he did in the competition, his daughter Taylor follows his stairs when he started sports and athletics. It affects Daisy's weight and face, the mother gladly said "You are sure you can't worry about yourself" because it criticizes how to find a man to find a better man to support him. He is very stable, he slipped into phone calls, and sometimes emails, so Daisy felt a child: anger, tired, depression. Narcissistic parentsDaisy's story - the adult son of an evil narcissist. In her most basic form, her mother saw her children as reflections of herself, not as separate individuals. As a result, a very clear girl, married to a rich man and now gains all glory and exacerbates you for the reach of race and race, which is now a jet. She grew up as her daughter. Single Margoraid is one of the academic achievements that did not understand or understand or did not understand, and are in close relationships with peaceful education with the mother who raped her.

Social networks and narcissism

If One of the things that children and youth of previous generations did not have was widespread social networks. When private moments, thoughts are written in a newspaper, photos in an album. Now they live forever online on websites like Facebook, Twitter and Instagram, exposed to the gaze, comment and judgment of the world. For many I like them, I post them, I share them, it affects their self-esteem, and for many these things feed their narcissism. In addition, it allowed them to take their narcissism to a new and harmful level. In the past, in the past, very few people have been interested in what you did at dinner, and during the last trip - the cellphone you made at the exhibition or bathroom, a new Dapie tattoo you have done at the end of your development. Social networks or even attacks are given to everyone, as if you want to see many of them. Some people definitely do this, especially if the poster is popular, but often these publications do not understand anyone but advertising. However, they are published. Why Because these posts and their reactions feed the narcissism of the post. People post bold photos or videos of themselves spitting into a tub of ice cream or punching someone. Behavior is ethics. Most importantly, the culture of social media teaches people that their feelings, thoughts, opinions, and actions are more about others than about themselves. It creates false meaning and relevance and reinforces the narcissism of a society full of self-portraits and emoticons. Children educated in this environment are prone to narcissism, especially if their parents or guardians cross the line between raising a child with high self-esteem and raising a narcissist. Personality development and narcissismThe desire of parents to boost their children's self-esteem is easy to understand, but according to psychologists Eddie Bromelman, Sander Thomas and Constantine Sedikides, when parents boost their children's self-esteem, it can easily lead to narcissism. Psychologists have been discussing personality formation for a long time. Is it genetic and therefore fixed from birth, or is it the result of a variable experience that varies according to circumstances? A third possibility is that it begins to be liquid in childhood and solidifies into adulthood. In this third option, the role of caregivers and learned behaviors are key to the development of healthy self-esteem or narcissism. According to Bromelman and his colleagues, there is a significant difference between self-esteem and narcissism. Yes, both depend on people's understanding of how they judge others, but that's where the similarities end, and the differences have a major impact on how everyone perceives their social world, themselves and others. For narcissists, this social world is structured in a vertical hierarchy with people above and below. Narcissists know no equals, but seek to reach the top by any means necessary to reinforce their delicate self-image by the captures of dominion. Any relationship is viewed as an opportunity that can be used to achieve the ultimate goal. On the other hand, people with high self-esteem see a parallel social world where everyone is on the same level. They focus on relationships rather than competition, and usually see these relationships as an end in themselves. There is a difference between self-supremacy (narcissism) and what people think is worthy (high self-esteem).Nargiz is an idiotAs a child progresses to narcissism, we often see the development of fear. After all, bullies share many of the same traits associated with narcissism, including a sense of superiority and a sense of legitimacy that masks vulnerability and often fear. They specialize in eliminating crime and usually prevent the abuses they create. Even worse, when a child complains to an adult, the teacher talks about the bully, it is often ignored because the bully plays the role of the victim, usually by the adults trying to deal with the situation. This begins a cycle of repeated abuse and unnecessary interventions that will soon undermine the victims' self-esteem.

Character traits indicating the potential for overbearing

Parents, Teachers and other health professionals, leaders, and educators need to identify the personality traits that lead to bullying. You'll find that these are all narcissistic traits that only strengthen the link between bullying and narcissism - Eddie Haskell. Stalkers work hard to make a positive impression on authorities like parents and teachers. However, if an adult observes for some time, he will notice that the same kindness is not shown to other children when the adults are not watching. This is a manipulation that should be controlled by adults.Know everything. This kid always thinks they are right without any proof to the contrary. This type of thinking is the result of the child's need to protect themselves from wrong or sensitive. This is a sign of deep insecurity. bluffs The child likes to tell others how great they are, refusing to hear other people's good news or sharing their own ideas or conclusions. A small child If an older child kisses when he normally doesn't, that's a bad sign. We are not talking about something that the child sees too much, but about a reaction to frustration. Because the innocent person feels no guilt or repentance, the child denies his innocence and blames someone else, maintaining this position for as long as possible, sometimes indefinitely. cruel king Like Baby Bowtie, the Tyrant King's attacks during the day are an antidote to frustration, not just deep insecurity, but a sense of entitlement. Malicious sperm is a child with an obvious lack of empathy who has the right to say or do atrocities to other children. They often don't know how or why what they say or do causes harm, and they usually don't care. This is a problem that needs to be solved in the near future. These personality traits indicate threatening behavior and are closely related to narcissistic personality disorder. Parents, teachers, and other health care providers should understand and recognize these symptoms to reduce any harm to the child or others.Don't raise a narcissistBased on their research, Bromelman and his colleagues concluded that child narcissism can be prevented while increasing self-esteem. For them: parents and teachers praise children's results without comparing them to their peers. For example, "Great job!" "you are the best!" Instead, it shows courage and efficiency. a sign of superiority Parents should encourage children to think about what they have in common with their peers and encourage them to be better than them. Finally, when a child suffers from low self-esteem, the adults in their life have to do two things: First, they have to assert the value of the child and help them get positive feedback on their low self-esteem. will not care Second, it helps the child accept what others are saying about him and take criticism as constructive feedback. Remember that all children deserve a safe and active childhood. By helping children overcome the kind of deeply ingrained insecurity that can lead to narcissism and bullying through a lack of empathy and appropriate responsibilities, we help ensure safety and effectiveness. Working with narcissistic siblingsFor narcissistic parents, it is almost inevitable that one or more children will also be narcissistic. Children follow their parents 'behavior and learn to deal with the world around them by modeling this behavior and building basic traits into their personality. The father does not feel too sympathetic, he feels good and teaches his children how "normal" people behave, and then the child internalizes them. This is exacerbated by the other parent, who usually takes on the role of an enabler or "flying monkey," often continuing the dynamic by rescuing the narcissist, apologizing, and defending his or her behavior. And after the death of the narcissistic father, it continues. Of course, not all narcissistic children become narcissistic. Some rebel against the narcissistic parent and are usually victimized by the family, while the narcissistic child appears to be loved, receiving what little love and attention a narcissistic parent can offer, and the protection offered by internal escape. monkey.

Yes they are trying to catch you

If you If your brother hurts you intentionally for no reason, you are not paranoid. They are out to catch you. The defining characteristic of narcissistic siblings is that they will do anything necessary to hurt you. It had nothing to do with anything he did or said other than a lack of parental love. They see it as a limited resource and you as a competition. They go out of their way to make sure they understand you and you don't. This type of bullying is designed to weaken their condition in the family, such as strangers without love, attention or support, and abuse is often ignored by a narcissistic father or ignores the apology that he is rewarded and rewarded. When you understand that a brother or sister of narcissism is a difficult task, especially because they do not grow and parents will never help because they do not grow and risk evaluating their behavior or conditions. Thus, it transitions to adulthood, where the once-aggressive intimidation tactics become more refined, sophisticated and effective. After all, they will not share the inheritance with you. Here's what you can expect from your narcissistic sibling: They will betray you somehow. They will use you in every way. They lie to you through proxy, silence, obscurity and misrepresentation. They hide important family information. They will judge you harshly and often hypocritically. Proximity to family can be very hostile to you, but not to others. They show complete disrespect for important events and milestones in their lives. They quarrel with you, assuming you don't know what you're talking about until you try to talk to them about something meaningful. Nothing changes in adulthoodYou would think that things would change when you grew up. After all, you and your brother are adults with adult responsibilities, so isn't it time to give up all childish behavior? If you're dating someone healthy like you, the answer is probably yes. However, you are not dating a healthy person. You are dealing with a narcissist who is an adult, and you are dealing with the trauma of developing narcissism that can lead to adulthood. Her feelings for her narcissistic brother today are rooted in the therapy she received in her youth. For example, if you feel anxiety around you, it's because part of you is waiting to be attacked. The pain of the past is still there, and when you are faced with an aggressor, even if there is no immediate threat, you feel the fight or flight response. And if his wild brother treated him well, he would always take care of himself. Your new civilization is an action, a way to hide the abuses of the past, but you rarely realize that deep down all the enmity and aggression is still hiding beneath the surface. Dealing with narcissistic siblings or parentsWhether he's a narcissistic brother or a father or both, all you need to remember is that they are ultimately narcissists. It means they are in it, they want and see themselves as superiors, and they will do terrible things to keep that illusion. Who they are, what they are, you cannot change them. You can change it too. Keep in mind that all relationships, including family relationships, are better. Of course, you have a biological relationship with narcissism that left you from your birthplace when you make this trip ahead as the possibility of leaving a violent family member. Breaking ties is not an act of betrayal. You comment, stay away, let the abuse happen and rule the abuser's life. You will be surprised how easy it is to breathe. This is an act of self-preservation on your part. If you feel the need to save the relationship, treat your narcissistic sibling as you would any other narcissist:Set and enforce boundaries for honest and clear communication, preferably in writing. Remember that children's tricks can limit information about you. The less information they have about you, the less likely they are to attack you. Share your relationship by keeping friends and colleagues away from your narcissistic brother. This denies the possibility that something terrible will happen to the narcissist and poison the well. Note that you owe them nothing and you don't have to agree or accept everything they need. Remember that their accusations against you are simply a projection of how they look and feel themselves.

We now have a basic understanding of the characteristics of narcissism and its social correlations in general. Let's take a closer look at how a relationship develops between a narcissist and an unsuspecting victim. Let's go back to our example with Mark and Claire. Part of the plan is for Mark to make Claire feel like she found her unchanging prince charming by having an affair with a narcissist. It will be all for him and will fill him with love and affection. It will give you everything you need emotionally, and everything will be fine for a moment. Remember what they say: if it sounds too good to be true, it usually is. This initial stage is a false "honeymoon" aimed at establishing a constant relationship with Chlorine. It gives you everything you want sexually and everything else you need. A brand is like a drug and quickly becomes addicted without realizing it. Even the most respectable, strong, morally conscious and intelligent people still have dreams. Narcissists learn to get into their skin and tap into their innermost desires. When that happens, if you don't catch the signals and run as far as possible in the opposite direction, you're in your womb! Unfortunately, Claire has no traces of narcissism because she never met a narcissist who tried to manipulate her. He was never surrounded by people who were not as kind and caring as he was. She likes that Mark has shown his sensitive side and feels that he is helping her through her pain by letting her know how he feels. But over time, it gradually disappears and it seems as if it has never been there. The gentle guy might have turned into something else, but at that point, Claire is madly in love with Mark again and, even worse, trusts him. Start using emotional and mental games to gradually destroy your self-esteem and self-confidence. She shared her mistakes and problems with her friends and family and encouraged discussions between Claire and people she loved and respected. This slowly separates her from the people she once trusted and helps her trust Mark more and more. Otherwise, he will give what he needs until he does. The emotional games gradually tear Claire apart until she becomes a shadow of her former self. Narcissists may have already used the gas lighting technique or are just beginning to implement it. Sometimes you get an impression of a brand you knew when you met them, and it lasts for another time. But little by little you will understand that everything is not as it seems. One of the first things victims may notice about their situation is that narcissists ignore consistency and reciprocity because they don't care about what other people think or feel. Mark doesn't necessarily appreciate how his public behavior reflects Claire, and she can brag, brag, and flirt with other women in front of him. When she starts arguing with him about this behavior, he easily dismisses her and tells her that she is inventing something, another sign that he has been bitten. How far a victim goes depends on the victim. Some of them have been communicating for years. Later, the narcissist disappears and then periodically reappears, telling the victim that he is insecure about things and insecure about their relationship, possibly indicating that the victim made a mistake in the relationship they caused. At this stage, the narcissist is forced to use everything to cause pain and make the victim feel that they have to compensate for what they did. Finally the game ends anyway. Mark gets bored and Claire decides to move on. But for the most part, Narcissus didn't let him go for long, even if a long time passed between appearances. Depending on the strength of the chain with their victims, victims wait, wait, and pray the next time they see their narcissistic companions. The pain and emotional control are so deep that they don't know they can live any other way. When we think of women in relation to physical abuse, many people think that it is too easy to judge women, to assume that they have to go, they have to go ... The truth is, they have never experienced such emotional abuse. It is impossible to understand how much one man can distort the reality of another through the manipulation of a wild couple. Victims of abuse often remember denying that there was a problem in the relationship or being so convinced that they are enduring the bullying and blaming themselves for what happened. This is a stern but true reality. Never judge a victim of abuse until you know what you are talking about. However, we must all realize that each of us is unique and we all have different strengths and weaknesses. How many times have you heard that from someone who didn't think they were going to fall in love? If you've been a victim of narcissistic abuse, it's important not to internalize a feeling like "stupid". The thing is, they do nothing in life but improve and manipulate others. They are professionals and experts. You are not stupid because you are human and feel. You have just met someone who knows how to properly apply your common human decency and kindness. After the cycle of abuse ended, she was finally freed from the narcissistic relationship , I hope he appreciates the fact that he was lucky to be released. Many fans never get what they need and want from a romantic partner in their life, and die unhappy and lonely. The emotional distress and lasting effects experienced by a victim of narcissistic abuse. In the next section, we will discuss the emotional disorder associated with ending a relationship with a narcissist and the long-term effects of the experience.

You can Say whether the person you are in a relationship with is a narcissist or not by their behavior during the relationship. Ideally, you should know if your boyfriend, girlfriend, or even friend has narcissistic tendencies so that you can break up with him before he gets too involved. Here are ten things a narcissist always does in a relationship.I will try to love youAs we mentioned throughout the book, narcissists can be very charming when they want something from you. When you are in a relationship with someone, they will go out of their way to make you feel special at first, so that they trust you to the point of losing their mind. He wants you to serve until you reach your goal. Narcissists are especially attentive and feel you are at the center of their world. If someone puts you on a pedestal in the early stages of your relationship, you should look at their reactions to see if they fail.It makes you feel worthlessAfter spending a long time with a narcissist, you realize that if you have a misunderstanding or quarrel, your first instinct is to let them go and make them feel worthless. He will criticize you for such a reluctant tone that makes you feel dehumanized. When you disagree with normal people, you always feel that your opinion matters, but a narcissist doesn't. Everything a narcissist says about you, even if you are attractive, is somehow turned into negative traits, and the narcissist pretends to be "holy" for tolerating those traits.Monopolize your conversationsNarcissists love the look of people, so they use it to talk about themselves. Whenever one tries to speak, the subject always changes and suddenly one talks about them. It's never a two-way conversation with a narcissist unless he's trying to manipulate you into thinking he's caring about you. There comes a time when he tries to hear his opinion or acknowledge his feelings. If you start telling something that happened to you at work, you will never finish because the story begins before you finish your story. If you comment on certain threads, your comments will be ignored, rejected, and unnecessarily edited. It's beyond youFrom the very beginning of the relationship, the narcissist begins to undermine his boundaries. You will understand that this is an invasion of your personal space and that it is not fair to ask you to never win. He even lends your personal belongings and money and does not return them, and when you pray, he tells you that he does not know that it is so important to you; The idea is to make people look bad by insisting on restrictions that the most competent people think are reasonable. break the rulesA narcissist defies the rules of their relationships and other social situations without moderation. The problem is that sometimes we are initially attracted to thugs because they seem “bad” or “rebellious,” but these traits are signs of narcissism. A person who violates social norms certainly violates the rules of relationships, because relationships are essentially social contracts. If someone tries to seduce you, but you find that they cross the line during the first interaction, give terrible advice, ignore traffic rules, etc., you can be sure that you are dealing with a narcissist. I will try to change youWhen you are in a relationship with someone, they (often unintentionally) blame you. However, in dealing with a narcissist, the narcissist will make a significant and intentional effort to change the narcissist, and often it will not improve him. I try to break you up and make you more of a servant. You will be susceptible to offers until the last minute. Every objective observer can say that you are under his control. It causes you to lose your sense of identity and eventually becomes a mere sequel. When you leave the relationship, it will be difficult for you to understand who you are as a person because he will define and redefine you throughout the relationship. I will prove him rightNarcissus shows the framework for most of his union. At first it may seem that he charms her with his generosity and compassion, but then he will see his own truth raise his ugly head. We look forward to priority treatment and hope you will make it a priority in your life (before a career or family). He has a clear distinction between what he offers and what he expects and wants to be at the center of his universe. I will try to isolate youAny narcissist who tries to control you will find that you have a support system of friends and family that will not hold you back or hurt you. One of the things he does when he falsifies feelings and gains confidence is he tries to isolate you. He asks you not to take anyone every time you pass by. He is lying to put a wedge between you and your friends. It will create a conflict between you and your family members, so you will trust them less. If you leave him out of his support system, he will have freedom and you will not have a chance against him. manipulation.

Chapter Eight

How to regain control

Regaining Taking control of your life after being bullied can seem difficult. But with the right advice and using the right resources, you can effectively restore your strength and regain your happiness. Yes, you are wanted. Yes, you have allowed this narcissist into your life for years. After years of isolation, abuse and surveillance, it takes a long time to get your life back on track. These steps will help you control your life and take revenge on the narcissist. Get a negative system. Like it or not, when you break up with a narcissist, you will have a lot of negativity in your system.

This alcoholism develops and tries to make them shut up and end the relationship. You tried to understand the narcissist who hurt you. It is time to leave all this darkness and leave the place where life is reborn. Writing a journal, sharing your story with friends, or hiring a therapist are some of the things you can do to prevent trauma. Storytelling can be helpful, especially if you have a listening partner to sort out your confusing thoughts. It helps him become stronger because he can finally be true to himself. Alternatively, you can do mental and physical exercises like yoga or dancing. It helps get rid of toxins and change the mind in a positive way. Make an event check. Although control may seem trivial, gathering experiences of control and abuse will help you understand what you have done and assess your growth: you will not allow yourself to return to the Being in this position. Such a memory makes you proud of your courage to leave him and hope for a fruitful life. You understand that now you can live as a free person and not return to violence. Listen to yourself, get used to it, your inner voice is the best tool available to you to resolve any situation. It shows how to act beautifully without lying. Even in times of great pain and despair, your inner voice tells you how to find a way out. According to Morph, Horvath, and Torchetti (2011), the main reason narcissists manipulate you is because they work with external stimuli in your brain to distort your internal stimuli. They acted for selfish reasons and controlled their brain activity for various reasons. However, by listening to your inner voice, you can recognize the situation and know when to move forward, stop, or reject what is being said. He will lead you to a new life and redemption where you will be free and understand yourself better. This will help you never fall in love with a toxic person. Organize your time and space Keeping your space clean and tidy is best because it gives you enough time to absorb everything that will come to you. As his kingdom crumbles, he becomes depressed when he registers in his mind that he needs to do more. As mentioned before, clutter allows you to organize your space and be alone with the things that matter to you. You will find that your brain responds positively to living in a clean environment. You will be more determined and ready to face each new day. An interruption can blur your mind and thinking. You can make a good daily schedule in which the most important tasks are distributed during the hours of the day when you are usually busy. active.Communicate with family and friendsAs already mentioned, narcissists often isolate their victims from their loved ones and friends. They may no longer understand you and may even think you hate them. You have tried many times because your attitude towards them has changed. Maybe some of them are trying to tell you that you are bad in your relationship, but you are always denying their feelings and trying to protect your narcissistic partner who should protect them from any attacks. Because he relies on Nargis for all his social needs, he finds it difficult to get along with people. However, the truth is that your loved ones will always be happy to talk to you, spend time and share with you.Be patient: take your timeThe worst mistake you can make is judging yourself and thinking that you are not moving fast enough to get out of the hole and forget about your narcissist. You shouldn't be too hard on yourself, instead you should understand that treatment needs time to be effective. Also each person needs different time periods to do something about it. Depending on the depth of the abuse or the length of the toxic compound, recovery may take more or less time. Recovery time is unlimited. Remember that your tormentor has already torn you away from the most valuable people and hobbies. They felt lonely and lost without them. As such, recovery can take some time and it is your responsibility to be kind and patient with yourself during treatment. The main thing is not to immediately jump into another relationship. It can interrupt your thinking and take time to heal. As a result, the next statement will be loaded directly and will not be healthy.Able to overcome everything. Depending on the depth of the abuse or the length of the toxic compound, recovery may take more or less time. Recovery time is unlimited. Remember that your tormentor has already torn you away from the most valuable people and hobbies. They felt lonely and lost without them. So recovery can take some time and your challenge is to be kind to yourself and be Treatment of the diseased ring. The main thing is not to rush into another relationship right away. It can interrupt your thinking and take time to heal. As a result, the next statement will be loaded directly and will not be healthy. Understand and forgive yourselfAllowing such a toxic person to be in your life so long can leave you feeling attacked. However, true healing and empowerment requires accepting a relationship with a highly toxic person who has intentionally harmed them. Admit that you have been deceived and mistreated. Trying to please them and show them that you understand, you will not see red flags. They also played to their strengths against him: making sure he had a good job, was well organized, receptive to ideas, and financially stable. You never deserve it and it is wrong to use it. Once you've acknowledged it, forgive yourself, knowing it wasn't your fault. Forgiveness is the most important thing right now. It doesn't matter how much time, energy, well-being or money you have lost. You have to forgive yourself and move on. It doesn't matter why you stayed so long, it doesn't matter why you were deceived. It happened before and you will be forgiven for it later. to search. Acquisition of knowledge: independent workIt is difficult to understand what cruelty he suffered and what to do next. For a long time, you only learned to look at the world through the eyes of an aggressor. Now he is confused and wonders where to start. Try to be more aware of your emotional well-being. There are many articles and online courses to help you with this. Knowledge is power, and increasing it never goes out of style.Change your focusHaving been mocked for so long, it's easy to slip back into his thoughts. These are aspects of cognitive shock and dissatisfaction that prevent proper recovery. The reason your mind pushes you is because you want to understand certain things and process the emotions associated with them. You don't have to dwell on these thoughts about the past and take advantage of the present. You can take one step forward and two steps back. Train your mind to be in the present and future of your choice. To increase the motivation for these endeavors, you need to update your dreams and look beautiful this time around. Think about the thoughts and things you wanted for yourself before you became a narcissist. Think about how badly you want them and increase your desire to achieve them. It's a shift from focus to perspective and a shift from your status from victim to hero. Although he is suffering, he may be surprised to find that after recovery he has become a self-absorbed, conscious, whole and whole man.Take back your life, pick up your story, understand what you know and heal yourselfAfter doing all this, you have to rule your life. You have already confessed that you have benefited and forgiven yourself. That's not enough, now you have to take the last step to become the pilot of your life. The thing is to clear your mind so that you can accept that your partner is intentionally hurting you and is a poisonous person. You have to admit that you are frustrated that they allow you to get hurt again and again. You don't listen to your instincts. They took your human qualities and used them against you. The truth is, you played a role in this relationship, whether it was love or empathy. In addition to acknowledging that they played a role in this, you must also acknowledge your role in forgiveness. At one point in the relationship, I felt angry but didn't pay attention to what I might have. Maybe because I expected it to work, I like them or sympathize with them. Therefore, by identifying yourself with the facts and accepting this fact, it will be easier for you to forgive yourself. To heal yourself, you must remove all historical suffering. You want lasting results. In doing so, it is important to eradicate unresolved pain, create a sense of inner stability, and restore a deep bond with hope. Where it goes depends on how much you want to let go of the pain of the past. Know that this is the right path to healing, and although it may take longer than expected, with dedication and persistence, you will eventually succeed. I'm sorryEven if her relationship with the narcissist has become violent, she can still have real and strong feelings for him. You loved him or liked the thought of him and you first got to know him when you went through the phase of love explosion where he reflected the desire of your heart. You like this idea quickly erased by the narcissus left behind, looking at you with the face of the person you loved as if suddenly this loved one has become possessed. You deserve the opportunity to mourn this relationship. Even if the person you loved was never a real person, he was real to you, and therefore you must allow yourself to cry. If it weren't for the loser, I would cry for the lack of relationship he deserved when he fell in love with narcissus. Pain includes five stages that occur, although they may not be linear. Pain also comes and goes, and even if one day you feel better, you will suddenly be surprised when you realize that you still miss the narcissist. This is normal, and pain is one of those things that never disappear entirely; you will learn to live with it. The first stage of illness is denial. You tell yourself that a relationship doesn't have to end.

You can try to convince yourself that what happened in your relationship does not guarantee a break. This is to protect against the pain you will feel when you officially finish. So go through anger. At this point, recognize the truth in front of you: the narcissus was violent. At this point, you realize the A narcissist is what he is and it hurts you. The thought of an abuser or criminal listening to him is enough to anger him. Third, discussion is negotiation. At this point, the anger has subsided a bit and you are telling yourself that there are ways or reasons to save the relationship. You tell yourself that if you try a little harder or harder, the abuse will no longer happen. Just keep the relationship going, tell yourself, try to get along with it if your coin ends up feeling good, like deciding that you're willing to be a martyr for the narcissist because you love him. This way you reach a state of depression. Here you know the relationship is over. You see things never add up and you destroy the faith you once had. You will finally be accepted At this point, even if you don't accept what happened or that your relationship ended, accept the decision and don't try to fight it again.BehaviorTrauma, especially abuse from someone you love and trust, can be very traumatic. Sometimes this is hard for you to do, or some of your narcissistic insecurities are too ingrained to get rid of. You may not have a clear idea of where to go for treatment and feel you need guidance. Whether you treat abuse well or badly, you can overcome it by seeking treatment. Everyone in this world can benefit from healing techniques. Therapy helps to learn to better solve problems, deal with negativity, reflect on and sometimes sharply traumatic events. What happened to the narcissist can certainly be considered traumatic, and don't hesitate to seek therapy if you feel it would be helpful. Having a familiar expert on your page, tells you what you feel in the healing process without judgment. You will have a man who can invent a true and valuable thought of why you do it or what you do with you and keep your hand while healing. This can be valuable, especially if your partner is particularly aggressive or struggling with thoughts of harming you, attempting suicide, or mental health problems. If you think seeing therapy is a good choice for you, start by asking your family doctor for a referral in your area, or you can search for therapists in your area online. Don't despair because you think treatment is stigmatized: There's nothing wrong with self-care, even if it requires the involvement of a professional. Remember, if you break your ankle, if you go to the doctor, no one will think or see that you are struggling with mental health. If you've suggested it, you can do it, don't let others make you feel like you're making the wrong decision.reportsThis is personal hygiene, but it is very important to be worthy of your category. Statements are small phrases that you repeat in moments of weakness or when you think you might have made the wrong decision to help you stay determined in those moments. As you create affirmations and use them regularly, you can read them to help you transform your negative thoughts into more effective beliefs. The accent has three key components: it should be positive, contemporary and focused on you. Keeping it positive means that you think about the positive aspects that are enough to change your attitude towards something. Fulfillment in the present tense means that you are now asserting that it is true. It gives you control over yourself. At the end of the day, you control yourself and only you, and reminding yourself of what you need to do or how you feel at a bad time helps. As long as these three conditions are met, all is well. Here are some examples of statements from those involved in narcissistic bullying: Competence and respect. I am happy with who I am now and accept me with all my flaws. An imperfect is perfectly reasonable, and I accept it. Every day, every hour, I am one step closer to healing and the next step in my journey. Even in the face of difficulties, it is always worthwhile to take the next step. My perception of reality is accurate and reliable, and I have to believe everything that happens. I'm as good as I am today, but I always have to strive to improve tomorrow.

Chapter Nine

Freourself from manipulation

You Stay away from narcissistic people because staying with them for a long time is not for you. However, there are situations when a narcissist is such an important part of a person's life that leaving him is completely impractical. For example, your wife could be your children, family members or classmates. In such cases, you can try to keep as much distance between them as possible while at the same time trying to minimize the damage to your children, other family members or your career. If their lives are still disconnected, you can break up with them, get away from them and completely avoid communication. Remember, they don't really care about you, so don't worry too much about how they will feel after that. Don't worry about too many details of why you're leaving. Remember that if you take the time to make excuses, they will try to prevent you from doing so. Bursting into a public place and never returning. Despite their stubbornness, don't accept them as friends and move on. Some psychologists recommend leaving the narcissist on the phone because it is impossible to know what a face-to-face meeting will be like. Avoiding contact with a narcissist, tell him you are not welcome at home and block his number on your phone. If you open a small window, you will find your way back into your life. Don't always say goodbye Just say your word and get out.There will always be mutual friends who will talk back to the narcissist, dump him and tell you you were wrong. These friends may intend well, but they certainly do not fully understand how much they have suffered under the rule of the narcissist. With them, you have to explain that the narcissist is an ungrateful person, and mentioning this during a conversation will cost you the friendship. Tell them you don't want to hear about the narcissist's life and if they are still talking to him, don't tell him anything about you. When you leave Narges for the day, write down exactly why you left. Write in a notebook the reasons for your decision and all the reasons why being with him was terrible for you. The thing is, when a narcissist comes into her life and she tries to deal with him, she can check her diary and remember why it's so important to stay away from him. We talked about gas lighting, how a manipulative narcissist can make her question her own mental health, so recording her thoughts and feelings at the same time helps her stay true. If you can get away from a narcissist, hopefully he will move forward quickly, find someone less annoying and leave you alone. Because narcissists never care about you, they won't obsess you, so don't doubt your decision when you see them move so fast that you might end up single. Better to be alone than with someone who takes life. Ignore NarcisonA narcissist lives to evoke emotional responses from people because he gives them power over his mind. When narcissism causes you to lose control of your emotions, it gives you great pleasure. When a narcissist verbally attacks you, ignoring them will drive you crazy. You have to understand that narcissists love attention, so ignoring them will hurt them more than anything else. They must be known and recognized. That's why they start with conflict. When a narcissist attacks you and destroys your life, your instinct is to attack with anger and emotion, but if you do, you are just playing into their hands. At first, it is not clear, but in the end you will feel that ignore narcissism is much more pleasing to him, because even the audience outdoors, even for the audience in the outdoors, is an adult who wants to be with people, he will treat everything. Nurses will ask you to rule and rule yourself, but you must remember that people cannot take your strength. You have to give it to him. Narcissists can only rule you if you give them control. As we mentioned before, if you play the narcissistic game, you will lose and then it can take over. Ignoring narcissists, you shamelessly refuse to play, so you will never get close to your life. If a narcissist is neglected, it hurts. Remember that you are doing this for yourself and your peace of mind. When choosing to ignore a narcissist, don't worry about the consequences of their lack of attention. If you ignore your narcissistic ex, don't chase him on social media to see if he's unhappy. Now that she has regained control, she needs to focus on detoxifying Narcissus 'influence and learn to be more cautious in the future. If a narcissist is a constant presence in your life, they are on your list of ignoring, so you need to teach yourself to improve. Ignoring a narcissist is more than avoiding responding to their sarcasm. It's about learning not to worry about your own opinions and criticisms. The first step is to stop responding to their comments, even if they hurt you, but you have to work on yourself to get to the point where what they say just washes away like water. Make a conscious effort not to give any meaning or significance to your words and actions. Consider them destructive actions and consider all actions against you unjust. That way they can cause you less pain.When you ignore a narcissist, you have to take care of your own safety. Some narcissists become aggressive or aggressive when you turn their attention away, so be careful not to be with them without a witness. Ignoring narcissists makes them feel uncontrollable, and when you despair of regaining control, you never know how crazy they are. You have to be very careful and intelligent because Narcissus will rule you again. Ignore them no matter how hard they hit you, don't even give up. Preparation for a vacation-Knowing that you can't change the person with a narcissistic personality disorder, you need to be willing to leave the relationship. Here are some things to do while you are getting ready or soon after you move. You will need support for this. Trust a friend or relative who knows you wouldn't trust your narcissistic significant other. Only after years of emotional abuse by a narcissist do you feel lost. You can trust someone you know. Find ways to regain self-worth and self-worth after years of emotional and verbal abuse. Remember your courage and avoid attacking and controlling people in the future. However, if you go, remember that he can take care of all his friends and do anything to make him a bad man. As someone with a narcissistic personality disorder, you cannot be seen as a villain. You need praise, affection and support from friends. Join a support group like CodyBents Anonymous with people who understand what's going on. They can help you heal.Establish an privacy policy and keep it to yourself and on your own. The treatment takes time and if you have a relationship during that time you are manipulated to get it back. Before you can see them, you need to gain confidence and self-esteem. It takes years and it's best not to search again if possible. Consult a therapist before traveling. You need all the support you can get, so build those relationships first. When you make the final decision to stop, stop! Naman Don't give yourself a chance to manipulate yourself. beware You are dealing with a dangerous person. Many people with a narcissistic personality disorder can be aggressive and angry and not know what is going on. If you feel a risk, take the necessary steps to protect yourself. When you go, you should bring your family and friends. In the worst case, you should notify the resettlement authorities and ask them to check. Beware of revenge Narcissists are known for revenge and compassion. Be prepared to emotionally expect something, but don't let it affect your new life without being narcissistic. If it comes out after you leave, don't open it. If possible, follow a non-contact policy for at least a year. Rebuilding a relationship with a narcissistDoors close and narcissists leave your life. But not from your spirit. What they do and say can stay with you for a while, even if it doesn't affect their self-esteem. Escape is hard, and now it will be hard to get away and start healing. Disengagement is key to retention and start of treatment. You need to separate yourself from everything you thought you knew about him and everything you felt about him. Leave the squad. Step 1: Stop blaming yourself for what went wrong and start blaming the narcissist for not being able to love you. Look at the connection between his personality and who he is as a person with a narcissistic personality disorder. Step 2: When you end a relationship, you go through stages of mourning, just like when someone dies. At this time, anger appears. You are angry at the way he treats you, because of your madness. Step 3: This is your platform. It's about how strong you are now. At this stage, you are thinking positive thoughts. You feel good about what you did. You have lost the love you once had for him, and now you can't bear to see him. Spend more time with friends and build a new life. Step 4: Publish! Success! Now you are concentrating on yourself and your life. You rarely think about him. You become physically and emotionally disconnected from the narcissist you may meet.

Find out If you explain a completely different story, then this is happening. We understand that the end of the story is quite positive. Of course, there will be pain and suffering, but you will overcome them. This is not the end of most narcissistic relationships. Here are some alternative results you can avoid. Even after you end the relationship and move on, the narcissist will find ways to continue to cheat on you. A narcissist accuses you of lying. They accuse you of doing something. He could also face charges. You are not recovering emotionally. You live depressed, lonely, resigned.At this stage, people lose jobs, family and friends. Abuse of psychoactive substances is possible. You lose interest in everything. Nothing gives more hope or joy. You are more prone to stress and depression. Living with a narcissist, we often underestimate the toxicity we have lived with all these years. Too many toxins in your body and you can kill yourself. Stress increases cortisol and weakens the immune system. Stress can increase blood sugar and blood pressure. It can lead to heart attack, cancer, depression, stroke and digestive disorders. There is also drug addiction and self-medication - narcissistic physical abuse. Although people who experience domestic violence do not have narcissistic personality disorder, some people with NPD may experience domestic violence. That's why we're paying so much attention to safety this season. be careful to stay informed Live your life, but don't take unnecessary risks. Unfortunately, some people in this situation cannot endure the stress, pain, abuse, loss of self-esteem and feel that they have no purpose and no value. They commit suicide. Never underestimate the toxicity of a full detox narcissus.

A close The author noted that parents need to ensure that their children have experience in keeping pets. Animals teach us about nature, life, death and responsibility. Animals raise questions. They make us understand why a hamster eats its young, why a snake torments its food, or why a domestic cat, even if it is not hungry, is still hunting. There are lessons in nature. Having a pet puts these lessons in the living room or at least in the yard. When trying to regain your thoughts, you should consider one thing: imagine what animals think. The best part about it is that it makes us think. Based on this process, we can ask deeper questions, such as about the nature of thought and whether nonhuman animals act like us. Or your thoughts may be as subtle as wondering why the kitten is looking in a certain direction or what it is thinking when we put its hand under the blanket. The second task is to imagine what your animals would say if they knew English. This performance follows well from the previous performance. Now that you've covered the trends and instincts associated with the concept of human thinking, you may be wondering how your kitten (or any other animal) would express themselves if it could speak English. Do you speak in complete or partial sentences? What thoughts do you want to convey to your owners? The third task is an attempt to communicate with animals. Again, this performance ties in well with the previous ones. Once you've thought about what an animal can think and feel and how it communicates, you need to look at how you communicate with your pet. It allows you to explore the nature of communication and its linguistic nature. Of course, language communication is often meaningless. An exception may be the word commands "sit" and "speak" for the dog type. It's a parrot - it's a language. . The fourth step is to try to understand what type of interaction the owner's pet wants and needs. The advantage of this method is the direct study of the individuality of the animal. This logical feature will help you listen to your pet's wishes and expectations. When you think about what this creature wants and needs so much, think about how important it is to the various aspects of your life. Think about what you do for the people in your life. Think about how much effort you put in to get what others expect of you. Consider how much control you have over this fact. Think about why you are doing this to your pets or others. Think about your desire to do something for others. Think about the level of control that comes to your mind in different situations. The fifth step is to give the animal what it wants and needs. This sounds obvious, but the extra goal is to realize that you are choosing to do something for another living being. This is not a unique feature. This activity should last a lifetime of your pet. If there is something related to the treatment of your pet, you may think that you have decided to do something with your pet because the animal needs or wants something. Recognize that you control what you do for others. The sixth step is to consider the quality of life of your pet. Many of the above measures lead to discussions about quality of life. It is worth knowing what kind of life is worth living. It is difficult for humans to answer this question, but pets can represent the basic needs of any animal, including humans. Consider improving the quality of life of your pet. It makes you think about what qualities you want and expect in your life. To what extent should your quality of life control certain aspects of your life? To what extent have you lost control of your relationship with the narcissist? What exactly is needed for repayment? How will you improve your quality of life to regain it? Once you've identified specific instances of things you don't have control over, and about which you want to regain, you can set up these activities to help you feel that sense of control. In the meantime, if you still can't find exactly what you need, try the following. No matter who you are in a relationship with, they give you a sense of control and acceptance of what you have no control over. Like gardening, pets, and hiking, it raises questions about nature. Why do certain plants grow in certain types of soil? On what does the color of the flower depend? Why aren't our tomatoes as good as store-bought tomatoes? Gardening is a way to learn about nature, be ashamed of nature and connect with nature. Playing in the potting soil is also an activity. Children have to dig in the ground. Take a look at the sand, chips, and everything a playground has to offer. It is useful to know the difference between one kind of landscape and another. You will learn interesting things about the differences between soil types and why some plants grow in one type of soil and not another. Remember, when I was in a relationship with a narcissist, it was like being put in the wrong country. You couldn't grow up there, the environment is bad You are not getting proper nutrition. The daffodil was like a plant that was picked without dividing anything and giving nothing back. The second task is to look for seeds and think about which plants will grow best in your conditions Again, compare your situation with the importance of certain conditions for the growth of certain plants. Note that a seed, no matter how strong it is, will not grow in a certain climate. His relationship with the narcissist was like a seed planted in the wrong place. You didn't reach your full potential while you were there. Of course, the third stage is sowing. Touch the floor. Learn to plant something. Mark what you have planted. Share your achievements with others. Be proud of what you have done. Remember that you are in control of everything that is under your control. Check the location, the terrain, the water and whatever you decide to hire. You can't control the weather, but you can control where your plant grows. After landing, you will find that you control the size of your environment. The fourth step is to measure the height. It's amazing to watch the development. By recording the growth of your plant, you can see an evolution (changes over time, not Darwin's theory). See the difference day after day and week after week. Height measurement. Count the leaves in recognition of your contribution to development. You limited their ability to sow. The fifth step is to remove weeds. The concept of weeds as a metaphor has already been introduced in a certain way. A comparison of the narcissistic abuse you have experienced, and the performance of plants consuming nutrients from other plants. With this comparison, separate the weeds from the garden so that the plants you want to grow do not suffer abuse. Whenever you weed, remember to remove narcissus plants from the garden so that the plants can grow quietly. The sixth job is cultivating individual plants and studying the healing properties of some plants. Surprise yourself by using different plants. Think, if we only use the resources we have, we can grow everything we need to heal in this world. You can also find some herbs to help you relax. Relaxation can help you heal. You can also find herbs that heal your body and help restore your emotions. When everyone is healthy, the body and mind are better. The seventh step is to observe insects. Keep your garden clean. Collect earthworms Free ladybugs on your rose bushes. Play with bugs, also known as rallies. Feel like the owner of your domain. Find strength in yourself and be kind to him. Don't be narcissistic, but master the things that matter to you. Find control over your tender nature. The eighth step is to respect the root. Whether you're planting tubers like potatoes or pulling weeds, looking at the roots is fascinating. Game using root words. Look at the root with a magnifying glass. Think about what a root is and think about the importance of roots in the garden and in life. Remember that your roots are more important than any daffodils to which you add your branches. The ninth step is cleaning. The garden is messy, but organization is key. Don't forget to take steps to keep your garden clean. Keeping order in the garden gives a sense of order in life. Consider the relationship between aesthetic and practical boundaries. Nargis may have understood aesthetics in her life, but she did not understand boundaries. Also install fences that look good in your garden and know that both are good. The tenth step is the use of garden tools. Using tools can help you control the situation. Learning how to handle a garden tool can be just as (or more) rewarding than learning how to handle any kind of tool you can imagine.

If you can control the things in your hands, you can control the thoughts in your mind. Gardening and caring for pets is not enough to regain lost control, but they are just the beginning. Think about all the things you can control. You don't lose control. The narcissists you were with made you think you are. You will find that activities like pets and gardening remind you of how much control you have. Practice these things often. If you don't like these activities, find someone you like. Find another way to use the tool. Find another way to see how much life depends on you hands.

Chapter Ten

Conclusion

Congratulations, great: you have reached the end of the book! This is an important first step to recognizing the possible abuse of a narcissist in your life. Questioning your relationship requires time and effort, which is the first step. This is the beginning of an acknowledgment of the crimes he has suffered and such a great step should be recognized and celebrated. The first step is to identify the narcissist. Remember the common traits and warning signs of a traveling narcissist. Be aware of the red flags, recognize them immediately and trust your gut when you feel something is bothering you. You should always trust your gut as it is often the first warning of error. Remember the signs of bullying and ways to deal with the damage that narcissists are trying to cause. If you remember to use the gray stone and protect yourself from the storm of rage and narcissistic outbursts or try to share it, you will survive. You have survived your situation and can protect yourself with the tools in this book to arm yourself. If you feel physically insecure in your relationship, remember that you can always ask for help. If you feel this is your best choice right now, there are domestic violence phone lines that can help you find resources and help. Most importantly, make sure you get treatment and try to do what is best for you. Don't be afraid to ask for help and don't be ashamed of your narcissistic actions. They will not think badly of you. Remember your health during this difficult time. Ending a relationship makes you last. Seeking help and support to survive makes you resilient. You are a warrior and do not want to deny and accept the abuse the narcissist has tried to cause you. You are not broken, unworthy, worthless or weak. you are strongYou survived. Remember that you can fear the unknown and the future. To fear something means to acknowledge the uncertainty and danger of the chosen path, but true courage means trying to go it yourself. One-day trip, hourly, minute-by-minute or step-by-step as needed. If you stumble, fall and make a mistake somewhere along the way, get up, clean your knees and move on. Accidents and mistakes happen and you still deserve to stay. The end of your journey is still waiting for you. Good luck on this journey, you deserve the joy and peace of having finally reached the other side of this long and winding road.

Milton Keynes UK
Ingram Content Group UK Ltd.
UKHW021133231023
431175UK00015B/1024

9 781804 771860